Stripples

Donna Lynn

Thomas

DEDICATION

This book is dedicated to teachers, whose gifts affect us in so many amazing ways.

To my first and most important teacher, my mother, Mary Louise Smith Brooks, who, along with so many other things, taught me how to sew.

To George Mayer, one of my favorite high school teachers, who taught one of my favorite subjects—geometry. I couldn't do what I do without it.

To Jessie MacDonald and Marion Shafer, who first taught me to quilt through their book *Let's Make a Patchwork Quilt.* I felt honored to meet Jessie briefly before she passed away.

To my dear husband, Terry, and sons, Joe and Pete, who teach me every day how wonderful life is with them.

CREDITS

Editor-in-Chief _____ Barbara Weiland
Technical Editor _____ Ursula Reikes
Managing Editor _____ Greg Sharp
Copy Editor _____ Liz McGehee
Proofreader _____ Leslie Phillips
Illustrator _____ Laurel Strand
Illustration Assistant _____ Lisa McKenney
Photographer _____ Brent Kane
Photographer's Assistant _____ Richard Lipshay
Design Director _____ Judy Petry
Text and Cover Designer _____ Amy Shayne
Production Assistant _____ Claudia L'Heureux

Thomas, Donna Lynn,
    Stripples / Donna Lynn Thomas.
        p.   cm.
    ISBN 1-56477-124-5
    1. Patchwork—Patterns. 2. Rotary cutting. 3. Patchwork quilts.
I. Title.
TT835.T463   1995
746.46—dc20   95-32907
                                                                 CIP

Printed in the United States of America
00 99 98 97 96 95   6 5 4 3 2 1

ACKNOWLEDGMENTS

As always, there are many people who contribute to the writing of a book. Each one of these people deserves special accolades for their tireless efforts.

A billion thanks to the pattern testers, who help ensure the patterns are as error free as humanly possible. They carefully search out both little glitches and glaring errors. Many of these ladies finished their quilts in time for them to be photographed. Thank you so much Rachel Childress, Dee Glenn, Ursula Reikes, Robin Chambers, Deb Rose, Mildred Gerdes, Kari Lane, Patti Stanley, Linda Kittle, Sharon Larsen, Gabriel Pursell, Beth Wagenaar and Roxanne Carter.

As we all know, it's not a quilt until it's quilted, and I am blessed with some talented quilters. Ann Woodward, Aline Duerr, and Norma Jean Rohman are some of the most gifted hand quilters I've had the privilege to know. They breathe life into my quilt tops with their beautiful handwork. Kari Lane and Betty Gilliam are true artists with their machines. The work they do with their creativity and ingenuity leaves me speechless. Heartfelt thanks to each of you.

Thanks to my friend, Sally Schneider. Her book *Painless Borders* helped me come up with some painless borders of my own. These are reflected in some of the patterns in this book.

One special lady, Marion Shelton, is on everyone's favorite people list. She keeps everyone happy with her warm smile, wonderful voice, and beautiful heart.

One last, big thanks to Ursula Reikes, my technical editor for two books now.

Stripples
©1995 by Donna Lynn Thomas
That Patchwork Place, Inc.,
PO Box 118, Bothell, WA 98041-0118 USA

Mission Statement

We are dedicated to providing quality products that encourage creativity and promote self-esteem in our customers and our employees.
We strive to make a difference in the lives we touch.

That Patchwork Place is an employee-owned, financially secure company.

Table of Contents

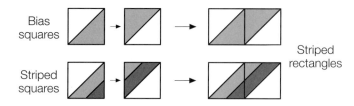

Introduction

What in the world are "stripples"? Actually, it's a made-up word that my mother and I came up with when we were brainstorming a title for this book. We tossed around key words and concepts that applied to the techniques in the book. Somewhere out of the highly charged air popped the word stripples—short for bias-stripped, striped rectangles (say that real fast several times and see what you come up with!).

Basically, a stripple is a striped rectangle. There are many examples of striped rectangles in both traditional and contemporary block designs. Until now, they have been tediously pieced from individual rotary-cut pieces or template-marked pieces. As a result, they were difficult and frustrating to work with because their size was rarely accurate after sewing and pressing. We would cut parallelograms (not much fun), and then sew the bias edges of triangles onto the bias edges of the parallelogram. After the bias seams were pressed, we'd hold our breath to see how far off the rectangle was.

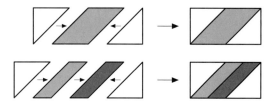

Never one for frustration, I realized one day that a striped rectangle is nothing more than two bias squares or striped squares sewn together. Rather than do all that piecing, I decided it would be much easier to make two bias squares and sew them together—a little unorthodox but certainly easier on the blood pressure. I'd been using bias strip piecing to make bias squares and striped squares for years. It seemed to follow that if I could use bias strip piecing to make the two bias squares, then I

could surely use it to make the complete rectangle itself and skip the step of cutting and sewing two bias squares together. Thus striped rectangles—stripples—were born.

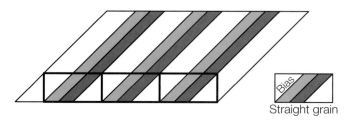

Stripples will show you a new way to piece these rectangles, using bias strip-piecing techniques. Anyone who has done straight-grain strip piecing to make units for a simple Ninepatch and other types of blocks is well aware of the benefits of strip piecing. Not only is the assembly faster but the accuracy is greater. Bias strip piecing is based on the same concept of sewing strips together and cutting presewn units from the completed strip unit. Bias strip piecing is used anytime the seam in a unit must be on the bias and the edge of the unit on the straight grain.

Instead of using strips cut on the straight grain of fabric, we use strips cut on the bias. The resulting strip unit is called a bias strip unit, and finished squares or rectangles can be cut from these units. The key to the success of this method is that the sewing and pressing are done before the units are cut. As a result, each and every square or rectangle is perfect in size without any distortions.

The next problem I had to address was how to figure the width to cut the bias strips. Regular rotary rulers are used to measure a specific width from one side of the strip to the other. Because of some basic facts of geometry, the end of the bias strip at the edge of the rectangle is not measurable in $1/8$" increments. This was a problem because I wanted to cut strips that measure a specific size on the outside edge of the rectangle so I could match them to squares and triangles in a block.

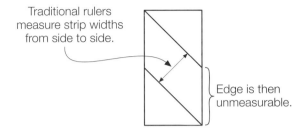

Traditional rulers measure strip widths from side to side.

Edge is then unmeasurable.

So I designed a ruler to do this and named it the Bias Stripper. It measures the width of bias strips at the edge of the unit. All you need to know is the finished size you want on the edge. It is not limited to use with striped rectangles but applies equally well to all bias strip piecing used to make bias squares, striped bias squares, and other units. It should make bias strip piecing more accessible to those of us who do not have degrees in higher math!

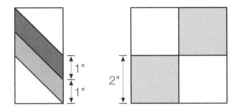

As you read and work through *Stripples*, you will learn new methods for cutting and sewing bias strip units to make striped rectangles as well as bias squares and striped squares. Study the quilts in the Gallery to identify the striped rectangles in each quilt. As you begin to recognize them, you should be able to understand how much easier it is to assemble the blocks when you cut most of the pieces as presewn squares and rectangles. There are twelve quilts with striped rectangles in this book for you to make. Some of the patterns also use striped squares and bias squares. A thirteenth quilt, added just for fun, uses the leftovers generated from the other quilts. I hope you find that bias strip piecing revolutionizes the way you make your quilts just as it has mine. Enjoy!

Equipment and Supplies

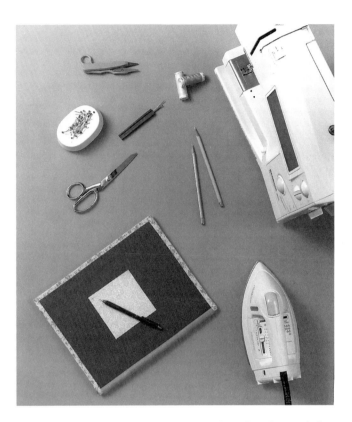

Sewing Machine. You need a simple straight-stitch sewing machine in good working order to piece a quilt top. Use a size 70/10 or 80/12 needle and replace it with each new quilt or when you hear a popping noise every time the needle pierces the fabric. Set your machine at about 12 stitches per inch or setting #2 on foreign machines.

Thread. Use a high-quality 100% cotton thread if it is available. Cotton-covered polyester is an adequate substitute. If most of the fabrics are dark, I use a dark gray thread and, conversely, if most of the fabrics are light, I use a natural, cream, or very light gray thread.

Regular Sewing Supplies. Items such as a good set of fabric shears, silk pins, thread clips, seam ripper, sewing needles, quilting needles, and quilting thread should be part of your basic quiltmaking sewing kit.

Sandpaper Board and Pencils. These are invaluable tools for accurately marking fabric. You can easily make a sandpaper board by adhering very fine sandpaper to a hard surface, such as wood, cardboard, poster board, or a self-sticking needlework mounting board. The sandpaper grabs the fabric lightly and keeps it from slipping as you mark. You need a fine-line mechanical or sharp #2 lead pencil. Use colored pencils for marking on the wrong side of a busy print if a lead pencil does not show. Keep pencils sharp for accuracy.

Ironing Equipment. Good ironing supplies need not be fancy, just clean and operable. Use a traditional ironing board or a terry cloth towel on a heat-resistant surface. Set your iron for cotton. Keep these items near your sewing machine since you need to press frequently. Keep a plastic spray bottle filled with water handy.

Rotary Cutter and Mat. There are many brands and styles of rotary cutters available. The larger cutters are better for cutting through several layers of fabric.

Rotary cutters have extremely sharp blades. Handle them with care and respect. Never leave the blade exposed, even for a minute.

You need a specially designed rotary mat to use with your rotary cutter. If you try to cut on any other surface, you will ruin not only the cutting surface but also the cutting blade. An 18" x 24" mat is the minimum size you should have for general quiltmaking.

Store mats flat and avoid extreme hot or cold temperatures that can cause warping. Heat from a hot mug or high-intensity work lamp is enough to damage them. Never store them in a car for the same reason.

Rotary Rulers. A good rotary ruler is an invaluable tool and an absolute necessity for general rotary cutting. For general cutting of strips and simple shapes, there are a number of good rulers available. Look for the following features in a general-purpose ruler:

1. Choose a ruler made of hard, ⅛" thick acrylic.
2. Look for a ruler with a 1" grid all over and ⅛" markings on the grid lines. This is particularly important because many quilt patterns use ⅛" increments. This type of ruler is also needed to cut the striped rectangles used in the patterns in this book.
3. Select a ruler with 30°, 45°, and 60° lines. The corner of the ruler is the 90° guide.
4. If you can afford it, buy a 6" x 24" ruler. At the minimum, you should have a 6" x 12" ruler to perform most general cutting.

Along with a general-purpose ruler, there are a few special rulers you need for the bias strip-piecing techniques used in this and other books.

The first is the Bias Stripper™. Use this ruler only when cutting bias strips. Do not use it for general-purpose cutting because it has nonstandard measurements. It simplifies the process of cutting bias strips and takes the math and guesswork out of figuring bias-strip widths. See pages 16 and 17.

The Bias Square® ruler is a square cutting guide designed exclusively to cut bias squares from bias strip units. In addition to its basic function, it has become a wonderful tool for performing many other rotary-cutting functions. Designed by Nancy J. Martin, it is used in many books published by That Patchwork Place.

Mary Hickey's BiRangle™ is a useful tool for cutting striped rectangles from bias strip units. The clear rectangular markings make it easy to see the rectangle you are cutting. If you use it for cutting striped rectangles in this book, though, be sure to ignore the diagonal line on the ruler since it was designed for use with another technique. See Mary Hickey's *Angle Antics* and *Quick and Easy Quiltmaking* for information on her wonderful BiRangle techniques.

Judy Hopkins's ScrapMaster ruler is the ideal tool for cutting and resizing triangles from scraps of fabric. See *Rotary Roundup* and *Rotary Riot* for more ways to use the ScrapMaster.

The Bias Stripper, Bias Square, BiRangle, and ScrapMaster are all available from That Patchwork Place. While it's not absolutely necessary, a 15" square ruler is handy for cutting oversize pieces of fabric.

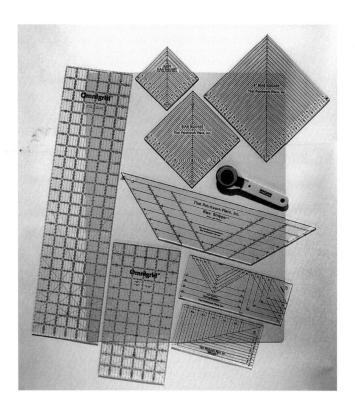

Fabrics

SELECTING FABRICS

There are two basic types of fabric palettes used in the patterns in this book. The first is a fixed palette. A limited number of fabric prints are chosen for the quilt, and each is assigned a specific place in the pattern. Usually there is one "anchor" fabric, which is the focal point of the quilt and generally, but not always, a multicolor print. It can be the border print, a background print, or the main print in the blocks. The remaining prints are selected to work with this print. Keep the quilt interesting by selecting fabrics with a variety of scales and prints. Don't be afraid to mix geometric prints, small and large florals, swirly prints, splashy and quiet prints, and plaids or checks. "Royal Beauty" on page 79 is a good example of a fixed palette. The light floral background fabric was the anchor fabric in this quilt.

The second type of fabric palette is my favorite—the scrappy palette. There are two ways to approach a scrappy quilt. A color-family scrap quilt is one in which a color family is assigned to a particular place in the quilt or quilt block. Then, a wide variety of prints within that color family are chosen and used randomly in the assigned position. "Pinwheel Shadow" on page 28 is a good example of a color-family scrap quilt. The color families are dark blue, soft green, and brick.

Another way to make a scrappy quilt is to assign dark and light values to specific positions in the quilt or block. "Crossing Paths" on page 80 is the only scrappy contrast palette in this book.

It is fun to combine elements of both approaches in one quilt. For instance, in "Radiance" on page 26, two blocks are made from each of a number of fixed palette combinations to produce a scrappy look. "Jack Frost" on page 53 is a blues-only quilt that uses a variety of dark and medium blues in assigned value positions in the blocks.

PREPARING FABRICS

It's a good idea to check all of your fabrics for bleeding before washing. Wash large pieces in the washer; wash smaller pieces, such as fat quarters, in the sink. Let the fabrics soak separately in warm water for about twenty minutes. If the water is clear or only mildly colored, the fabric is ready for washing; otherwise rinse again, several times if necessary, until the water remains clear. If the fabric still bleeds after several rinses with no sign of letting up, I recommend that you *not* use the fabric.

Dry the fabric on low heat until damp dry and then press with a hot iron. Gently straighten and refold your fabric, selvage to selvage, as it was folded when you bought it.

UNDERSTANDING FABRIC AND GRAIN LINE

When fabric is woven, the yarns used in the weaving process create different grain lines. These different grains have different abilities to stretch or "give." Fabric from the bolt has two finished edges, called the selvages. The lengthwise grain of fabric runs parallel to these two selvages and has little or no give. The crosswise grain of fabric runs from selvage to selvage and has a slight amount of give. Both crosswise and lengthwise grains are called the straight grain because they run parallel to woven yarns in the fabric. The true bias runs at a 45° angle to the lengthwise and crosswise grains and has a generous amount of give.

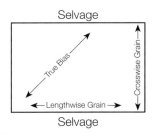

Generally, when making quilts, try to cut shapes as close to the straight grain as possible. Due to the quirks of mass production, few fabrics are printed on grain, and many are stretched off grain when rolled onto bolts for sale. You can sometimes straighten a piece of fabric that is badly off grain by holding opposite diagonal corners and gently pulling.

All strips, squares, and rectangles should be cut on the straight grain. Some shapes, such as triangles, cannot have all edges cut on grain. Therefore, it is a good idea to look at the position of the shape in the pattern and consider these guidelines when deciding which edges to cut on grain.

1. Place all edges on the perimeter of a quilt block on the straight grain so the block does not stretch out of shape.
2. Whenever possible, without violating rule 1, sew a bias edge to a straight edge to stabilize the seam.

Basic Rotary Cutting

CREATING AN EVEN CUTTING EDGE

To cut accurate strips from your fabric, you need to create an even cutting edge.

1. Lay the freshly pressed fabric on the rotary mat with the fold toward you and the selvages aligned at the top of the mat. If you are using a 12" long ruler, fold the fabric again to bring the first fold at the bottom up to the selvage edges at the top.

2. Place your rotary ruler just inside the raw edges of all fabric layers at the left-hand edge. (If you are left-handed, cut from the right edge of your fabric.) Place the edge of the Bias Square ruler on the bottom fold of the fabric and adjust the rotary ruler so that it is flush with the Bias Square. Aligning the Bias Square with the fold ensures a clean cut that is at right angles to the bottom fold and eliminates bent or V-shaped strips later.

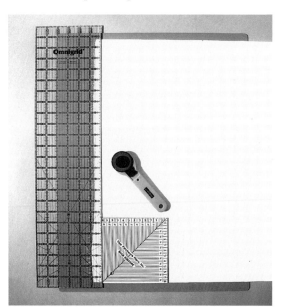

3. Hold the rotary ruler securely in place. Anchor it by placing your fingers or the palm of your hand on the mat, to the side of the ruler. Move the Bias Square aside. Cut away from yourself with firm, downward pressure, rolling the blade along the ruler's edge. Make one clean, firm cut from below the fold to above the selvages. It may be necessary to "walk" your hand up the ruler as you cut to keep it from shifting out of line. If you are not cutting through all the layers, exert a stronger downward pressure or check the blade for nicks or dullness. Sometimes, a seemingly dull blade simply needs cleaning with a clean, lint-free cloth and a drop of sewing-machine oil behind the guard.

Once you have an even cutting edge, you are ready to continue cutting.

> **TIP** *If you are left-handed, cut from right to left in all situations. Cutting from left to right will be awkward for you, resulting in inaccuracies and frustration.*

CUTTING STRIPS

Almost all rotary cutting begins with strips of fabric. Some strips are used whole, while others are cut crosswise into other shapes, such as squares, triangles, bars, and rectangles.

To cut a 2½"-wide strip, align the 2½" line of your ruler with the even cutting edge of the fabric. If you are right-handed, this edge will be on the left and you will cut fabric strips from left to right. If you are left-handed, this edge will be on the right and you will cut fabric strips from right to left. To prevent a bent strip, always align one of the ruler's horizontal lines with the fold at the bottom of the fabric. Cut the strip from bottom to top, away from yourself, as you did when cutting the first even edge.

In rotary cutting, the ¼"-wide seam allowances are included in the cut dimensions. Therefore, strips for strip piecing, squares, bars, and rectangles are always cut ½" wider than the finished measurements of the desired unit.

Cutting Squares

Cut strips the width of the square's cut size. Turn the strip and cut squares from the strips crosswise. Be sure to align a horizontal line of the ruler or Bias Square across the bottom of the strip before each cut.

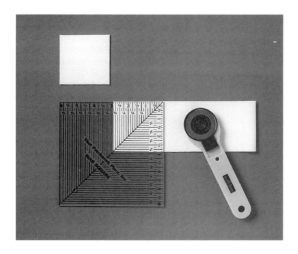

Cutting Bars and Rectangles

True rectangles are twice as tall as they are wide, for example, 2" x 4", 3" x 6", or 4" x 8". Bars are "stretched squares" of other dimensions, such as 2" x 6", 1" x 4", or 2" x 3". Rectangles and bars are cut from strips in the same manner.

Cut strips the width of the rectangle's or bar's cut size. Turn the strip and cut units the length of the rectangle or bar.

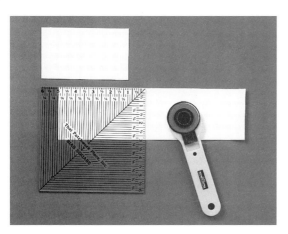

Cutting Half-Square Triangles

Make half-square triangles by cutting a square once diagonally, so the straight grain is on the two short edges. When these triangles are used in a block, the short edges fall at the outside edges of the block.

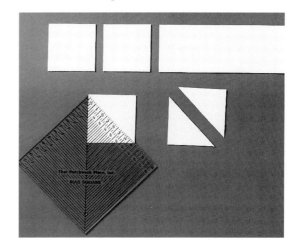

To determine the size of the square needed to yield two half-square triangles, including seam allowances, add ⅞" to the desired finished size of the short (straight-grain) edge of the triangle. Cut a square this size and then cut it in half on the diagonal.

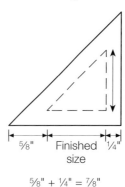

⅝" + ¼" = ⅞"

Sometimes, you may need to cut a few extra half-square triangles. Rather than cutting another strip or more squares, cut extra triangles from leftover fabric, or resize edge triangles from bias strip units, using Judy Hopkins's ScrapMaster tool. With the ScrapMaster, you can quick-cut individual half-square triangles without first cutting a square. The tool is marked for cutting a number of common sizes of half-square triangles. Please note that the cut dimensions of the triangles, not the finished sizes, are the sizes marked on the tool. When using the tool, remember the following guidelines:

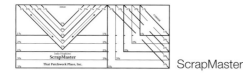

ScrapMaster

For 1" finished triangles, use the $1\frac{7}{8}$" lines.
For $1\frac{1}{2}$" finished triangles, use the $2\frac{3}{8}$" lines.
For 2" finished triangles, use the $2\frac{7}{8}$" lines.
For $2\frac{1}{2}$" finished triangles, use the $3\frac{3}{8}$" lines.
For 3" finished triangles, use the $3\frac{7}{8}$" lines.

To cut half-square triangles from edge triangles or fabric scraps:

1. Create a square corner on the straight grain of a piece of fabric, using the corner of the tool.

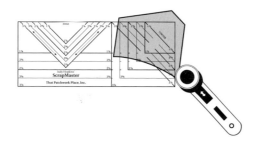

2. Align the corner of the fabric with the proper edge-triangle lines and cut along the straight edge of the tool to remove excess fabric.

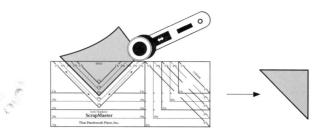

In addition to cutting half-square triangles, you can use the ScrapMaster in a number of other ways. Please see the package directions for more detailed uses, along with *Rotary Riot* and *Rotary Roundup* for accompanying patterns.

NUBBING HALF-SQUARE TRIANGLES

Nubbing triangle points removes excess fabric that extends beyond the $\frac{1}{4}$"-wide seam allowances, so that the edges of squares and triangles are easier to match for more accurate stitching. Even when sewing triangles, nubbing eliminates the need to go back and clip off the "dog ears" that remain after sewing a seam.

To nub half-square triangles, add $\frac{1}{2}$" to the finished size of the triangle's short side. For example, to nub a $1\frac{1}{2}$" finished-size triangle, place the Bias Square ruler on the triangle's corner at the 2" mark as shown in the diagram ($1\frac{1}{2}$" + $\frac{1}{2}$" = 2"). Cut off the tips that extend beyond the ruler edges.

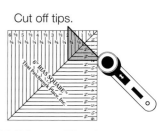

Cut off tips.

Half-Square Triangle

Nubbing can also be used to resize triangles that are too large for the ScrapMaster. Add $\frac{1}{2}$" to the desired finished size of the new triangle you want to cut. Use the Bias Square ruler to nub the triangle to this size, using the instructions above. Now rotate the triangle and cut the long edge to $\frac{1}{4}$" from the nubbed corners to provide an accurate seam. The triangle is now nubbed and resized to fit your requirements.

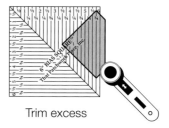

Trim excess

CUTTING QUARTER-SQUARE TRIANGLES

Make quarter-square triangles by cutting a square twice diagonally, so the straight grain is on the long edge in each resulting triangle. When these triangles are positioned in a block, the long edges are along the outer edges of the block. Quarter-square triangles are also used for the side setting triangles at the outer edges of diagonally set quilts.

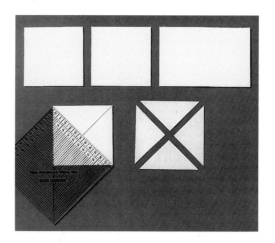

To compute the size of the square to cut, determine the finished size of the long (straight-grain) edge of the triangle. Add 1¼" to this measurement and cut a square this size. This square, when cut twice diagonally, will yield four triangles with the proper seam allowances included.

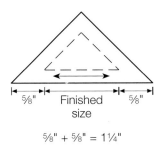

5/8" ← Finished size → 5/8"

5/8" + 5/8" = 1¼"

The size of the square to cut for side setting triangles is given in the quilt instructions, but it's a good idea to know how to calculate the correct size square in case you change the dimensions of the quilt. When setting blocks on the diagonal, you only know the finished size of the side setting triangle's short edge, which is equal to the finished size of the block. To cut quarter-square triangles, you need to know the finished side of the triangle's long edge. To determine this, multiply the block size by 1.414 and round up to the nearest ½"; then add 1¼" to this measurement. The triangles cut from a square this size will be slightly oversized and can be trimmed to size after setting them into the quilt.

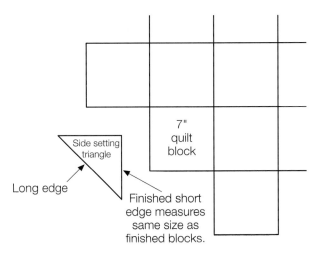

Long edge

Side setting triangle

7" quilt block

Finished short edge measures same size as finished blocks.

For example, to compute the side setting triangles for a quilt with 7" finished-size blocks:
1. Multiply the block size by 1.414: 7" x 1.414 (9.898"); round up to 10".
2. Add 1¼": 10" + 1¼" = 11¼"
3. Cut an 11¼" square for every four side setting triangles needed.

CUTTING OVERSIZE PIECES

When cutting oversize pieces of fabric, it's handy to have a 15" square ruler. If you do not have one or you need to cut pieces larger than 15", you can still use rulers you have on hand.
1. Align the long edge of your ruler even with the lower fold of the fabric, measuring the required distance from the even cut edge. Cut along the short edge of the ruler, perpendicular to the fold.

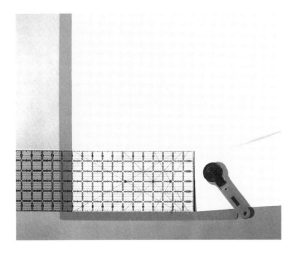

2. Turn your ruler, aligning the long edge with the short cut you just made. Be sure that a horizontal line on the ruler matches the fold to ensure a right-angle cut. Continue the cut up to the selvage edges.

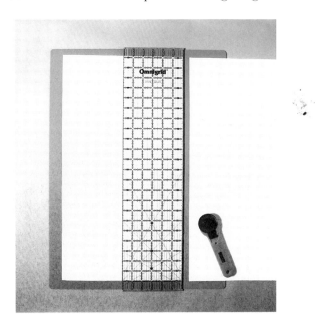

You are now ready to cut this piece of fabric into squares, rectangles, or whatever other shapes you need.

REUSING LARGE LEFTOVER PIECES

Rather than discard them, use larger leftover fabric pieces to cut extra strips, squares, and so on, for your quilt, or in a pinch, when a little extra fabric is needed due to error.

To cut strips from square or rectangular pieces:

1. Use a large square ruler to make a square corner with two clean-cut adjacent edges.

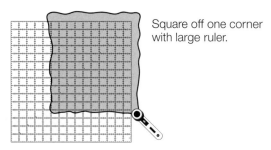

Square off one corner with large ruler.

2. Cut the fabric into strips as usual, then cut the strips into the shapes you need.

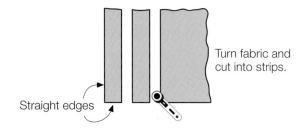

Turn fabric and cut into strips.

Straight edges

To cut strips from triangular pieces:

Square off two adjacent edges to create a straight-grain corner in the same manner described above. Cut the triangle into strips and then into the shapes you need.

Square up corner of triangle.

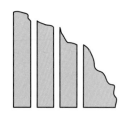

Cut into strips.

TIP *If you do not have a large square ruler, cut one edge on the straight grain. Then cut the adjacent edge, making sure a horizontal line on the ruler lies along the first clean-cut edge.*

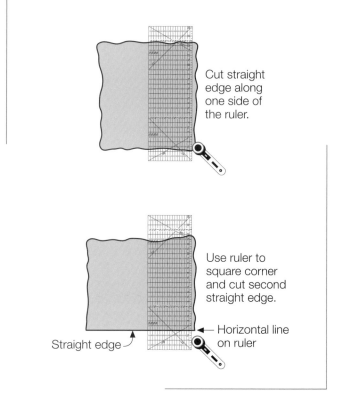

Cut straight edge along one side of the ruler.

Use ruler to square corner and cut second straight edge.

Straight edge

Horizontal line on ruler

Basic Stitching

SEWING AN ACCURATE SEAM ALLOWANCE

All cutting dimensions include ¼"-wide seam allowances. Therefore, it is imperative to sew an accurate seam. Otherwise, the impact of minute errors in the seam width increases with each subsequent seam.

Test the accuracy of your machine's ¼" guide, whether it is the edge of the presser foot or a marked line on the throat plate. Cut three strips of fabric, each 1½" x 3". Sew them together side by side using the ¼" guide. Align the edges and stitch slowly and carefully to test the machine—not you! When sewn and pressed, the center strip should measure exactly 1" wide if the guide is accurate.

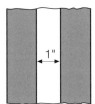

Center strip should measure a perfect 1" from seam to seam.

If the center strip does not measure exactly 1", you must create a new guide. The best solution is to buy a special ¼" presser foot for your machine. Many sewing machine manufacturers have responded to quilter's needs with new ¼" presser feet. Check with a local dealer to see if one is available for your machine. Generic ¼" presser feet are also available through quilt shops, sewing-supply stores, and mail-order catalogs. They fit most machines, but check first.

If a new presser foot is not possible, try shifting the position of your needle to the right if your center strip was too narrow or to the left if it was too wide. Conduct another strip test to check the accuracy of each needle position until you find the perfect position.

You can also create a new sewing guide by using layers of masking tape or a strip of adhesive-backed moleskin. To find the correct position for these guides, raise the presser foot on your machine. Then raise the unthreaded needle to its highest position. Cut a 2" x 6" piece of ¼" graph paper. Put the piece of paper under the presser-foot area and lower the needle into the graph paper, just barely to the right of the first ¼" grid line so that it is included in the dimension of the seam

allowance. Otherwise, the stitching would decrease the size of the finished area by a needle's width on each seam you sew.

Adjust the paper so it is running straight forward from the needle and is not angled to either the left or right. Lower the presser foot to hold the paper in place. Use a piece of tape to hold the left edge of the paper so it doesn't slip.

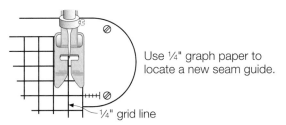

Use ¼" graph paper to locate a new seam guide.

¼" grid line

Stick a piece of masking tape or moleskin on the sewing machine along the right edge of the graph paper as shown below. Make sure it is in front and out of the way of the feed dogs. Make another strip test for this new guide. If it is not accurate, adjust it until you can sew an accurate strip test several times in a row. If you are using masking tape for your guide, build up the guide with several layers of tape to create a ridge that will help you guide the edge of the fabric.

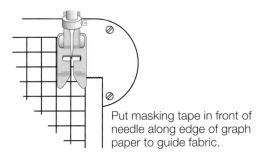

Put masking tape in front of needle along edge of graph paper to guide fabric.

PRESSING

There are two primary reasons for pressing seams in a particular direction: 1) so that the seams rest against each other (butt) at the intersections for sewing, and 2) so your completed block or quilt will lie flat and smooth. Pressing toward the darker fabric, which is a common instruction in quiltmaking, is a luxury you can consider after these two conditions are met.

Here are a few tips for pressing a seam crisply toward one side, without any pleats or puckers showing on the right side.

1. Press, don't iron. Pressing is the gentle lowering, pressing, and lifting of the iron along the length of a seam; ironing—moving the iron forcefully back and

forth along the seam—distorts it. Use an occasional spritz of water to press the fabric in the desired direction.

2. Always press the seam line flat after sewing, before pressing it in one direction. This relaxes and sets the thread, eases out any small puckers that result from stitching, and smooths out any fullness you may have eased in as you stitched.

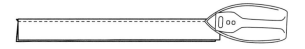

3. Press from the right side. Use the tip of the iron to gently press the top fabric over the seam allowance. With the seam allowance held in place by the ironing surface, it is easy to work the fabric over the narrow seam allowance. I find this method much easier than trying to use a big iron to press a narrow seam allowance over the fabric from the wrong side. In addition, working from the wrong side often results in messy, inaccurate pleats at the seam line.

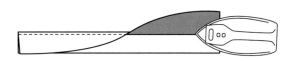

4. Press in the direction of the fabric's straight grain. When the straight grain runs along the seam, gentle pressing along the seam follows the straight grain. When the bias runs along the seam, gentle pressing at a 45° angle to the seam follows the straight grain. Do not press straight along a bias seam, or stretching and distortion will occur.

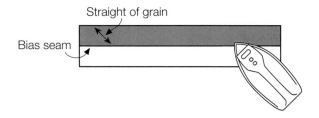

Straight of grain

Bias seam

5. Correct pressing mistakes by returning the unit to its original unpressed position, spritz the seam, press the incorrect crease out, and then press the seam in its new direction.

6. When assembling strip units, press seams one by one as they are sewn rather than waiting to press them all at once later. This is especially critical with bias strip units as they can easily stretch if you try to manipulate and press a mass of sewn strips. You'll also find that you can manage the construction of multiple-strip units far better if previously sewn seams are all neatly pressed and flat as you sew the next strip in place.

There are pressing instructions with each quilt plan in this book. The green arrows shown in the piecing diagrams indicate the direction to press the seams to ensure that the block goes together easily. Be sure to follow the directions carefully as I have tried to work out the best-possible pressing plan for each pattern.

STITCHING SEAMS

Machine stitching is usually done from raw edge to raw edge, except in a few special cases. Backstitching is unnecessary because all stitching is crossed by another seam. Even the outermost border seams are secured by the stitching used to attach the binding.

To stitch rotary-cut pieces together, place them right sides together, aligning the raw edges. Pins are not normally used for strips and simple piecing. It is important to sew slowly and accurately, keeping edges consistently aligned. All the accurate cutting methods mean nothing if the stitching is not accurate. Please see my books *A Perfect Match* and *Shortcuts: A Concise Guide to Rotary Cutting* for more extensive information on machine piecing, specialty seams, and more tips for accurate stitching.

MATCHING INTERSECTIONS

The easiest way to tightly match intersections is to press the seam allowances in opposite directions. In this way, a ridge is formed by each of the seam allowances, and these ridges can be pushed tightly against each other. This is called butting the seams.

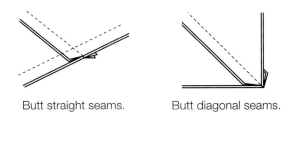

Butt straight seams.   Butt diagonal seams.

SEWING PARTIAL SEAMS

Sometimes, it is necessary to leave part of a seam unsewn. Usually, this is a situation where a block is built in a circular fashion around a central piece as shown in the block below.

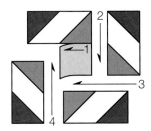

To avoid complicated piecing situations, sewing half of the first seam allows the second seam and each subsequent seam to be sewn in place completely. The diagram shows that with the first seam only half sewn, it is easy to sew the last seam. The final stitching completes the second half of the first seam. Backstitching is unnecessary when you overlap your beginning stitches with the last bit of stitching.

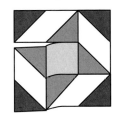

Sew second half of
first seam to finish block.

STRAIGHT-GRAIN STRIP PIECING

Straight-grain strip piecing is a technique that, in many cases, replaces the process of cutting and sewing individual squares, bars, and rectangles. The idea is to cut strips across the fabric width, sew the strips together, press them, and then cut the resulting strip unit into segments. The simple Ninepatch block is a good example.

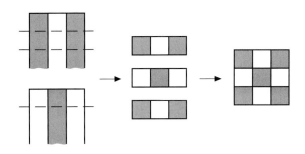

CHECKING YOUR WORK

As you stitch, it's a good idea to check the dimensions of the units you have just sewn to make sure they are the correct size. It is much easier to correct problems at each stage of construction rather than later when ripping (reverse stitching), correcting, and restitching becomes more complicated and involves more seams. Continue to check your work as you progress. Interior pieces should be the intended finished size, while the outer pieces should be the finished size plus $1/4$" for seam allowances.

When your blocks are completed, check them again, even though you may have checked your pieces as you worked. They should be accurate in size. Generally, discard any block that is too small to "fudge." Sometimes, if a block is too large, you can trim it down to size, using interior seams as guidelines.

Bias Strip Piecing

Bias strip piecing is a similar technique to straight-grain strip piecing except that the strips are cut on the bias grain instead of the straight grain of the fabric. The most common unit cut from bias strip units is the bias square, which is a square composed of two half-square triangles sewn together on their long edges. As a result, the straight grain lies on the edge of the square.

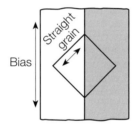

If you cut bias squares from straight-grain strip units, the outer edges of the square have bias edges. But, if you cut bias squares from strip units with bias edges (bias strips), the outer edges of the square have straight-grain edges.

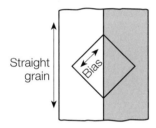

If you vary the width of the bias strips used in the strip units, you can easily cut other pieced units, such as striped squares and striped rectangles. Striped rectangles are used in every pattern in this book. Bias squares and striped squares are also found in some of the patterns.

Striped Rectangles   Striped Square

USING THE BIAS STRIPPER RULER

The Bias Stripper solves two problems quilters encounter with bias strip piecing.
1. Determining where to make the first bias cut on the fabric
2. Determining how wide to cut strips that include seam allowances

The new Bias Stripper helps you cut accurate bias strips without messy computations—the math is built into the ruler itself.

Cutting bias strips is simple when using the Bias Stripper ruler. It is specifically designed to look different from other rulers so that it will not be confused with standard rulers. Its longest edge has a $1/2$" margin to account for the two seams sewn on either side of a bias strip in a strip unit. Measurements are given in $1/8$" increments along the two short edges of the ruler, with continuous lines that run the length of the ruler every inch. A number of short lines on the ruler's inner area run parallel to the short edges. The ruler is easy to use by both left-handed and right-handed quilters.

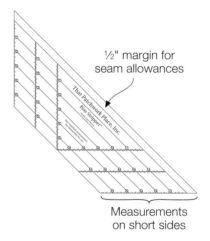

$1/2$" margin for seam allowances

Measurements on short sides

Warning: Do not use the Bias Stripper to cut straight-grain strips. The measurements along the short edges do not reflect the width of the strip from side to side! For example, strips cut at the $2\frac{3}{4}$" mark will not measure $2\frac{3}{4}$" wide.

DETERMINING BIAS STRIP WIDTHS

Bias strip widths are provided for each pattern in this book. However, you can use the Bias Stripper ruler to cut bias strips for any pieced square or rectangle, whether it is one of your own design or one adapted from a traditional pattern. You only need to know the finished sizes of your units to determine the correct cutting mark for cutting the bias strips.

To determine strip width for bias squares:

1. Determine the finished size of the bias square.
2. Add ¾" to this dimension and cut bias strips at this mark.
   Example:
   2" finished size + ¾" = 2¾" cutting mark

To determine strip width for striped squares and rectangles:

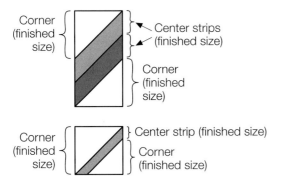

1. Determine the finished size of each center strip.
2. Cut bias strips for center strips at this mark.
   Example:
   1" finished size = 1" mark
3. Determine the finished size of the corners.
4. Add ¾" to this dimension and cut bias strips for the corners at this mark.
   Example:
   2" finished size + ¾" = 2¾" cutting mark

Making *Method One* Bias Strip Units

This is the original method designed by Nancy J. Martin and Marsha McCloskey to create bias squares. Even though it is used only to make bias squares, I find it an extremely useful technique to know.

CUTTING BIAS STRIPS

The bias grain of the fabric is found by cutting a straight-grain square in half on the diagonal. The resulting large half-square triangles have long bias edges from which you can cut bias strips.

Pair squares of the two prints with right sides together. If you are right-handed, place the short edge of the Bias Stripper on the upper left corner of the fabric squares, and the margin edge of the ruler along the diagonal of the squares. If you are left-handed, place the short edge of the ruler on the upper right corner of the fabric square. To create a bias cutting edge, cut across the diagonal of the squares from bottom to top, along the edge of the ruler.

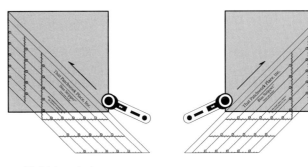

Right-handed   Left-handed

Rotate the lower pair of triangles to match the top pair and cut bias strips from each pair of triangles by aligning the required cutting mark on the diagonal bias cutting edge. The width of the bias strips is indicated in the instructions for each pattern.

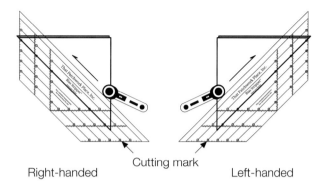

Right-handed   Cutting mark   Left-handed

SEWING BIAS STRIP UNITS

Pick up the bias strips in pairs as they were cut and sew them on their long edges. Press them as the arrows indicate in the pattern illustrations.

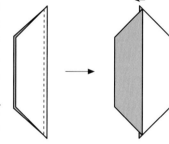

For maximum use of fabric, sew the bias strip pairs together into multiple bias strip units, keeping the units together according to length and aligning the points on one edge. Remember to press each seam as it is sewn rather than waiting and doing it all at once at the end. See "Pressing" on pages 13–14.

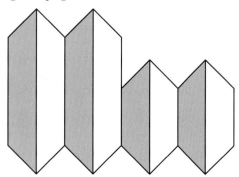

CUTTING BIAS SQUARES

Use a Bias Square ruler to cut bias squares from the sewn and pressed strip units. The Bias Square ruler has a diagonal line and ⅛" markings that meet at the center to form squares.

1. Begin at the lower end of the bias strip unit and position the diagonal line of the Bias Square ruler on the seam. The numbers on the ruler should be on the top.

2. To cut the first bias square from the lower points, make sure the desired square dimensions are just inside the raw edges at the bottom of the strip unit. Cut the top two edges of the bias square from raw edge to raw edge.

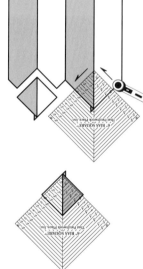

3. Turn the bias square and trim the remaining two raw edges to the proper size by aligning the markings on the Bias Square ruler with the clean-cut edges.

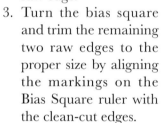

4. Continue cutting across the strip unit, moving from lowest point to lowest point systematically and from either left to right or right to left.

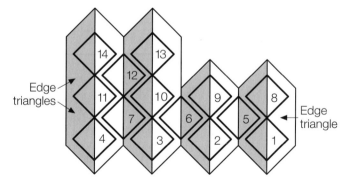

5. Leftover single triangles are created at the edges of the strip units. The number of edge triangles is reduced by increasing the number of pairs of bias strips in the strip unit. Even so, the edge triangles can be nubbed, resized, and sewn into bias squares if necessary. See "Nubbing Half-Square Triangles" on page 10.

Making *Method Two* Bias Strip Units

Use Method Two bias strip units to make all kinds of bias units, including bias squares, striped squares, and striped rectangles. Instead of cutting bias strips from squares of fabric as in Method One, cut bias strips from rectangular pieces of fabric, for example, a 9" x 42" piece of fabric. Sometimes, you don't need a full 42" piece and less is indicated in the pattern, such as a 9" x 34" piece. Only full bias strips are used to make strip units for striped squares and striped rectangles.

Use Method One and the large triangular corner pieces left over after cutting full bias strips to make additional bias squares. See page 22. You can also sew these pieces together to make an interesting back, or save them for another project.

CUTTING BIAS STRIPS

1. Layer one or more rectangles of fabric flat on the cutting mat, placing them either face up or face down as instructed in the pattern. Following the face up or face down direction is critical since you could end up with mirror-image strips. Do not fold the fabric(s). Selvages will be on the left and right. Once your fabric is positioned, remove the selvages.

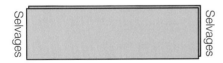

Note: If you are left-handed, lay the fabric on the mat so it faces in the opposite direction from the instructions in the pattern. For example, if the instructions tell you to place the fabric with the right side face up, place your fabric with the wrong side face up. You will also cut strips from the right-hand edge of the fabric. If you need to cut equal numbers of bias strips in both directions, it doesn't matter if you are left-handed or right-handed.

2. To make the first bias cut, align the short edge of the Bias Stripper ruler with the upper corner of the fabric layers. Cut the fabric along the edge of the ruler from bottom to top. Set aside the large triangular corner piece created by this first bias cut.

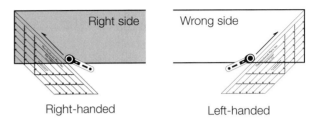

3. Cut bias strips from the layers of fabric by aligning the required cutting mark on the short edges of the Bias Stripper ruler with the cut edge of the fabric.

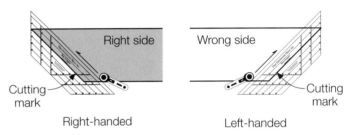

4. Continue cutting bias strips until you can no longer cut full bias strips (strips that run completely from the top side to the bottom side of the fabric). There will be another large triangular corner piece left over from this side of the fabric. Set it aside for now.

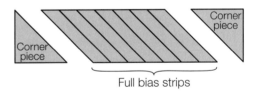

TIP Sometimes, the last full bias strip will be just a little short (clipped) on the lower corner. You can cut and use the strip as long as the clipped point is less than 1" high.

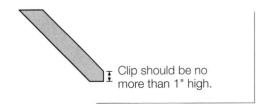

Clip should be no more than 1" high.

SEWING BIAS STRIP UNITS

Separate the layers of full bias strips and organize them as indicated in the pattern. If you have a clipped strip, lay the clipped end toward the bottom edge of the unit.

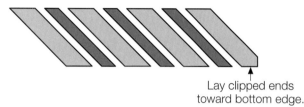

Lay clipped ends toward bottom edge.

Begin sewing the strips together, following the directions below.

1. Offset the strips when sewing. Begin stitching at the V, where the angled edges of the two strips intersect at the ¼"-wide seam allowance. This yields a strip unit that is even along the top edge and down one side, making it easy to cut it into squares and rectangles. If you do not offset the strips properly, your strip units will resemble a step ladder, which is very wasteful and difficult to cut.

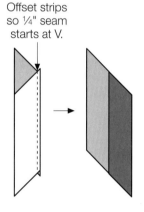

Offset strips so ¼" seam starts at V.

2. Always sew strips from the top of the strip unit to the bottom so that the top edge of the strip unit is aligned.

Sew strips from top to bottom.

> **TIP** *If the edges of your bias strips tend to separate as you sew the seam, despite your best efforts at sewing slowly and controlling the bias edges, the problem may be with the presser foot. In most cases, switching to a wider presser foot solves the problem. Of course, if you are using the edge of your presser foot as the ¼" seam guide, you need to establish a new guide. See "Sewing an Accurate Seam Allowance" on page 13 for help in creating a new guide. If a wider presser foot does not help, take the machine to your local dealer for help.*

3. If you need to take out a bias seam, be careful not to stretch it. Use a seam ripper to cut the thread every two to three stitches and lift the bias strips apart. Pulling the thread from the end of the seam can stretch the bias edges.

4. Press each seam before adding another strip onto the strip unit. When you are working with bias strips, it is difficult to press all the seams at once on a completed strip unit and still keep the unit straight. See "Pressing" on pages 13–14. Follow the pressing instructions provided with each pattern.

CUTTING STRIPED SQUARES

Only Method Two full bias strips are used for striped-square bias strip units.

1. Assemble the strip unit as instructed in the pattern. Position the strip unit on the cutting mat with the even edge toward you. Tilt the unit to the left or right as comfort dictates.

2. To cut striped squares, center the diagonal line of the Bias Square ruler on the center seam line of the striped square. Keep the required dimension of the square inside the bottom raw edge. Cut the striped square just as if it were a bias square. Then turn each cut striped square and trim the raw edges to size.

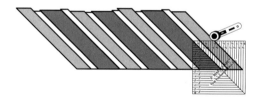

When striped squares are cut from the strip unit, tiny slivers of fabric are left over between each striped square, and small waste rectangles are left over between each pair of striped squares as in the diagram below. (The tiny slivers are not shown in the diagrams.) Save the edge triangles for another project. I have cut small bias squares from the waste rectangles and used them in miniature quilts.

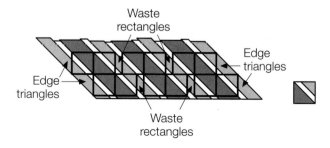

Waste rectangles

Edge triangles

Edge triangles

Waste rectangles

CUTTING STRIPED RECTANGLES

Only Method Two full bias strips are used for striped-rectangle bias strip units. Assemble the strip unit as instructed in the pattern. Position the strip unit on the cutting mat with the even edge toward you. Tilt the unit to the left or right as comfort dictates. Use a standard quilter's ruler or Mary Hickey's BiRangle ruler to cut rectangles.

If you are using a standard quilter's ruler, it should be at least 6" wide and marked with a 1" grid and $\frac{1}{8}$" markings along each grid line. Some people find it helpful to mark off the rectangle they are cutting with $\frac{1}{4}$"-wide masking tape on the top of the ruler. If you use the BiRangle ruler, ignore the diagonal line; it is meant as a guide for another technique.

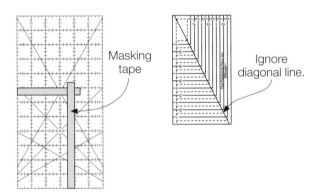

Masking tape

Ignore diagonal line.

1. Position the ruler on the strip unit, with the rectangular dimensions inside the bottom raw edge. Align the upper left corner of the ruler with the seam of what will be the upper left corner of the rectangle (arrow A). The ruler mark for the opposite lower right corner of the rectangle should be aligned with the seam that intersects that side of the rectangle (arrow B). Depending on the design of the rectangle, there may be one or more seams in between the two that intersect the rectangle corners. Do not worry about any placement for those interior seams. Concern yourself only with placing the ruler correctly over the seams that intersect the two corners.

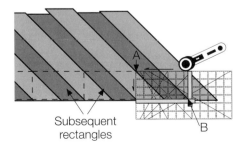

Subsequent rectangles

2. Cut the top long edge of the rectangle first and then the short side. If you are left-handed, cut the short side first, followed by the top edge. Do not cut too far up into the strip unit when cutting the short side, or you will cut into the rectangles to be cut above. An $\frac{1}{8}$" to $\frac{1}{4}$" cut above the ruler is okay.

3. Turn the rectangles around and trim the remaining two sides to the required size, just as with bias squares.

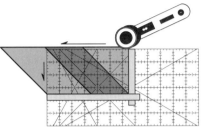

Trim last 2 sides of the rectangle.

4. Continue cutting rectangles across the bottom of the strip unit, just as with striped squares and bias squares. There will be small slivers of fabric left over between the rectangles; these are not shown in the pattern diagrams.

Place even edge toward you.

Note: If your strip unit slants to the right, move the masking-tape markers to the opposite side of the ruler and cut from left to right. If you use the BiRangle ruler, you need to turn the ruler over to cut the rectangles.

21

CUTTING BIAS SQUARES

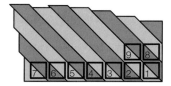

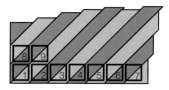

1. Assemble a Method Two bias strip unit, adding bias strips cut from leftover corner pieces. See step 3 in box below.

2. To cut bias squares from Method Two bias strip units, position the strip unit on the cutting mat with the even edge toward you. Tilt it to the left or right as comfort dictates, just as we slant paper at different angles when writing.

3. Beginning at the bottom even edge, align the diagonal line of the Bias Square ruler on the seam, keeping the square's dimensions inside the raw edges. Follow the directions on page 18 for cutting Method One bias squares. There will be slivers of fabric between each bias square. These slivers are not shown in the diagrams.

Note: If the strip unit slants to the left, begin cutting from the right in order to align the diagonal line of the ruler on the seams. If the strip unit slants to the right, begin cutting from the left for the same reason.

REUSING METHOD TWO CORNER TRIANGLES

Use the corner triangles left over from cutting and sewing Method Two bias strips to make additional bias squares. These triangles are no different than the ones cut from squares of fabric. The first corner pieces created when making the initial bias cutting edge in Method Two are ready "as is" to be cut into bias strips. The corner pieces left over from the other end of the fabric after the full bias strips are cut may be odd-shaped pieces and need to be "triangled up."

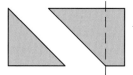

This piece needs "triangling up."

1. To do this, lay the short edge of the Bias Stripper on the diagonal edge of the odd-shaped corner piece, with the margin edge to the right, and the ruler point on the lower right edge. (Reverse these directions if you are left-handed.) Cut along the margin edge to create a large triangle.

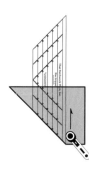

2. To cut the triangle into Method One bias strips, place the triangles right sides together. Align the bias edges (don't worry about the triangle corners) and follow directions on pages 17–18 for cutting Method One bias strips and bias squares.

3. You can also use bias strips cut from the corner pieces in conjunction with Method Two bias strip units. Cut the corner pieces into Method One bias strips as described above and add them to the full bias strip unit as shown. Sew from top to bottom and offset the strips ¼" as shown on page 20. The bottom edge of the strip unit will be uneven.

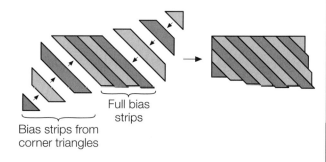

Bias strips from corner triangles

Full bias strips

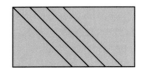

The Patterns

The striped rectangle is used in all the patterns in this book. Some of the patterns also make use of straight-grain strip-piecing techniques as well as other bias strip-piecing techniques. The information for the different techniques is included in the front section of the book. Since some or all of it may be different from anything you have done before, I strongly encourage you to read the front matter thoroughly before making any of the quilts.

All fabric requirements are based on 44"-wide fabric and include an allowance for shrinkage. If you are like me and tend to make at least one major cutting blooper with every quilt, buy an extra ¼ to ½ yard of each fabric! I have also found that a few of the newer fabrics do not measure a full 44" wide. This means that they may shrink to less than the 42" minimum width generally allowed for determining fabric requirements. Please check fabric widths at the point of purchase and again after you wash them so that you can buy extra yardage of any fabrics that are less than 42" wide.

In patterns that call for the use of fat quarters, it is assumed that the fat quarter measures no less than 17" x 21" after washing. If not, you may want to switch to ¼- or ⅜-yard pieces, depending on the number and width of the fabric pieces you need to cut.

Information for cutting bias strips is provided in easy-to-read charts. Each chart indicates the number and size of large fabric pieces to use, the direction to face the fabric pieces (when necessary) when cutting bias strips, the total number of bias strips needed from each fabric in each size, and the strip unit in which each strip will be used. Do not cut the large leftover corner triangles into Method One bias strips unless you are directed to do so. *Be sure your fabric faces in the direction indicated in the chart or written instructions.* Special instructions are given for left-handed quilters if they are needed, provided they are following the instructions for cutting bias strips found on page 19.

One other task you may want to complete before beginning the patterns is a bias strip test. In the front of the book, you learned how to test your seam guide with a straight-grain strip test. It's a good idea to practice cutting and sewing bias strips the first time on a set of test bias strips.

1. Cut a 5" x 10¼" piece of fabric on the straight grain.
2. Cut 3 full bias strips at the 1" mark, using the Bias Stripper.
3. Sew the 3 bias strips together side by side.

Cut 3 bias strips at 1" mark.　　　Sew them back together.

Press and check the completed strip unit for stretching and other problems. The center strip should be the same width as the 0 to 1" mark on the Bias Stripper. If not, you may want to check your ¼" guide and how well you are aligning the fabric with the guide when you sew.

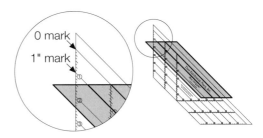

Center strip should measure at 1" mark on Bias Stripper.

Repeat the strip test until you feel comfortable cutting and sewing bias strips. Performing this test really helps sharpen your sewing and precision skills before cutting and sewing entire strip units for a quilt. I strongly encourage you to try it.

If you would like a little more practice beyond the strip test, turn to the "Radiance" quilt on page 40. The fabric requirements for this quilt are for making two blocks at a time. Make just two blocks to practice cutting and sewing bias strip units as well as cutting bias squares and striped rectangles on a small scale.

Pressing directions are very important for easy, accurate quilt assembly. The assembly diagrams contain green arrows indicating the direction in which to press the seam allowances. Your block will lie flat if properly pressed, but even more critical is to have the seams butt at the intersections for precise matching. I have tried to work out the best-possible pressing plan for each quilt. Sometimes, though, there is not a perfect plan for a particular design so I have chosen the best solution I could find. Please pay attention to the arrows—I think you will be pleasantly surprised at how much easier it is to assemble the quilt when pressing is worked out in advance and not attacked willy-nilly as you go.

In all the patterns, you will have corner triangles left over after cutting the required number of full bias strips. Some of the patterns use these leftover triangles for other parts of the quilt. Other patterns do not use them, and I routinely instruct you to use these pieces for a pieced backing or set them aside for another project. If I were reading this book, my first question would be a rather amused "What other project"? Well . . . for all of you who hate leftovers, I have provided one more pattern called, Another Project: Crossing Paths, based on the traditional Sawtooth Square block. I took leftover corner triangles from the patterns in this book, previous books, and class samples and gave them to my quilting friend Beth Wagenaar along with the block instructions, and she made the bed-size quilt shown on page 80. You can do the same with your leftover corner triangles. Collect them and make a lot of Sawtooth Square blocks later or make a few every time you accumulate a small stash of leftover corner triangles. In fact, any scrappy bias square pattern is a good place to use these leftovers.

GUIDE TO PATTERN RATINGS

Confident Beginner: Must feel comfortable using the rotary cutter to cut straight-grain strips and machine piecing strip units. One-cutter patterns use fewer and simpler bias strip units and are relatively easy to construct in a short amount of time.

Intermediate: Must be comfortable with the concept of bias strip piecing and machine piecing. These patterns use a moderate number of more intricate bias strip units. Block construction is more involved than one-cutter patterns.

Skilled: These patterns are for those who are very comfortable with bias strip piecing and machine piecing. They are more challenging in both the types and numbers of bias strip units required. Three-cutter patterns should delight more experienced quilters who are tired of the same old thing and want to try a new challenge.

READ ME

Please keep the following points in mind as you work your way through the patterns.

❑ Remember, do not use the Bias Stripper ruler for cutting straight-grain strips and units.
❑ Use a $\frac{1}{4}$"-wide seam allowance for all piecing.
❑ Press in the direction of the arrow unless otherwise indicated.
❑ Pay attention to the fabric direction in the charts when cutting full bias strips.
❑ Follow the piecing diagrams carefully for the proper orientation of pieced squares and rectangles.
❑ Don't rush—it's important to read the instructions as well as look at the diagrams.

❑ Follow the instructions on page 95 to add plain borders. Enough border strips are provided in the cutting instructions to piece the necessary border lengths for each quilt. Sew the strips end to end to make one long border strip. Then measure and cut borders from this unit as needed.

Note: If you prefer unpieced borders, you will need to purchase extra fabric and cut border strips from the lengthwise grain of the fabric.

Gears 'n Gadgets
by Donna Lynn Thomas,
1994, Lansing, Kansas,
40½" x 40½".

*Two colors of the same motif
appear by setting the blocks
together without sashings.
This simple but dynamic
design would be terrific in a
young man's room. Machine
quilted in copper metallic
thread by Kari Lane.
Directions begin on page 29.*

Midnight on the Prairie
by Rachel Childress,
1994, Leavenworth,
Kansas,
40½" x 40½".

*Rachel used a scrappy red,
blue, and gold palette, which
gives her quilt a completely
different look from mine. In
addition, she artfully changed
the use of contrast, giving
more depth and dimension to
the design. A light seems to
glow from behind and through
her quilt.*

Helix Stars
by Ursula Reikes,
1995, Redmond,
Washington,
53½" x 53½".

Ursula's eye for color and design really comes through in the periwinkle blue and warm gold prints she selected to go with the black multicolored print. The lighter diagonal bands of fabric give a slightly three-dimensional look to the design. The multicolored print frames the quilt beautifully. Directions begin on page 36.

Radiance
by Donna Lynn Thomas,
1994, Lansing, Kansas,
66½" x 66½".

Radiance is made two blocks at a time, using a dark, medium, and light trio of prints for each pair of blocks. The two blocks, although made from the same fabrics, are positive/negative versions of each other. What a wonderful opportunity to sit and play in your fabric stash, creating fabric trios from all your favorites! Machine quilted with bold diagonal cables by Kari Lane. Directions begin on page 40.

Garden Memories
**by Robin Chambers,
1994, Media,
Pennsylvania,
67½" x 67½".**
*Bright, cheerful prints make
this happy, breezy quilt perfect
for a sunroom and white
wicker furniture. Add
lemonade and a good book for
a perfect summer day.*

African Stars
**by Kari Lane,
1994, Lansing, Kansas,
52½" x 64½".**
*Kari's bold use of fabric is her
trademark. Truly an artist,
she has incorporated batiks,
fabrics from Africa, and some
of her own hand-painted
creations into this breathtak-
ing quilt. She used twenty of
the many blocks she made to
make a larger quilt.*

27

Pinwheel Shadow
by Donna Lynn Thomas,
1994, Lansing, Kansas,
44" x 52".

Rich, quiet, and peaceful, this quilt "needs" to be touched. Although the quilt is scrappy in nature, the single background print quiets and unifies the design while the border showcases a stunning print reminiscent of Monet or Renoir. Exquisite floral wreaths are quilted over the pinwheels. Hand quilted by Ann Woodward. Directions begin on page 33.

Cosmic Pinwheels
by Deirdre Glenn,
1994, Lansing, Kansas,
44" x 52".

Wow! Dee zapped electricity into her quilt through the use of hot colors that sizzle and pop. The gold flecks in the pink print are accentuated by the quilted gold metallic rays of light. Prairie points finish this quilt perfectly.

Color photo on
page 25.

Finished Quilt Size
40½" x 40½"

Finished Block Size
8" x 8"

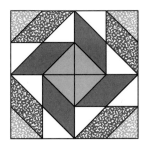

Gears 'n Gadgets

Dark green print

Medium green print

Dark red print

Medium red print

Background print

Materials: 44"-wide fabric

⅞ yd. dark green print
⅞ yd. medium green print
⅞ yd. dark red print
⅞ yd. medium red print
1⅛ yds. background print (includes inner border)
⅜ yd. binding
1⅜ yds. backing

CUTTING

All measurements include ¼"-wide seam allowances.

From *each* of the dark green, medium green, dark red, and medium red prints, cut:
4 strips, each 6" x 42"; crosscut into:
  8 pieces, each 6" x 17", for Strip Units I and II

From the background print, cut:
4 pieces, each 6" x 34", for Strip Units I and II
4 strips, each 2½" x 42", for inner border

From the fabric for binding, cut:
4 strips, each 2" x 42"

Refer to the instructions on page 19 for cutting Method Two bias strips.

Using the Bias Stripper, cut the number and size of full bias strips indicated in the chart. Cut all fabrics face down. If you are left-handed, cut all fabrics face up.

FABRIC	NO. OF PIECES	SIZE	CUTTING MARK	TOTAL NO. FULL BIAS STRIPS	STRIP UNIT
Dk. Green	8	6" x 17"	2"	32	I
Med. Green	8	6" x 17"	2¾"	24	I
Dk. Red	8	6" x 17"	2"	32	II
Med. Red	8	6" x 17"	2¾"	24	II
Background	4	6" x 34"	2¾"	32	I & II

Reserve the following leftover 6" corner triangles for the pieced border; set aside the remainder for a pieced backing or another project.
13 dark green, 14 medium green, 14 dark red, 13 medium red

PIECING THE BLOCKS

Refer to the instructions on pages 19–21 for making striped rectangles, and page 22 for reusing Method Two corner triangles. Press all seam allowances in the direction of the arrows unless otherwise instructed.

1. Assemble 8 Strip Unit I. Cut a total of 64 striped rectangles, each 2½" x 4½", from Strip Unit I.

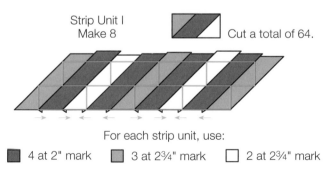

Strip Unit I
Make 8

Cut a total of 64.

For each strip unit, use:

■ 4 at 2" mark ■ 3 at 2¾" mark □ 2 at 2¾" mark

■ Dark green ■ Medium green   Dark red   Medium red □ Background

2. Assemble 8 Strip Unit II. Cut a total of 64 striped rectangles, each 2½" x 4½", from Strip Unit II.

Strip Unit II
Make 8

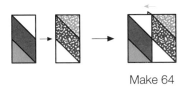

Cut a total of 64.

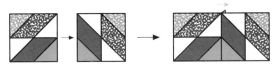

For each strip unit, use:

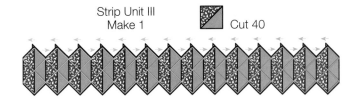 4 at 2" mark   3 at 2¾" mark   2 at 2¾" mark

For each strip unit, use:

4 at 2" mark   3 at 2¾" mark   2 at 2¾" mark

3. Sew a green striped rectangle to a red striped rectangle. Make 64 pairs of striped rectangles.

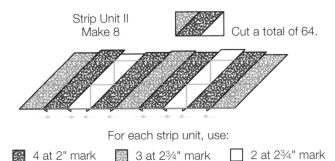

Make 64

4. Sew the pairs together to make 32 half blocks.

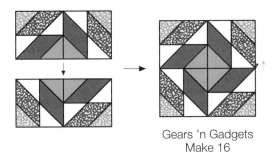

Make 32

5. Sew 2 half blocks together to complete a Gears 'n Gadgets block. Make 16 blocks.

Gears 'n Gadgets
Make 16

Assembling and Finishing the Quilt Top

1. Sew the blocks together in 4 horizontal rows of 4 blocks each as shown in the quilt plan on page 29. Rotate the blocks if necessary so that the seams butt when the blocks are joined. Press seams joining the blocks in opposite directions from row to row. Join the rows; press seams in either direction.
2. Attach the 2½"-wide inner border to the quilt top, following the directions for "Plain Borders" on page 95.
3. Pair a 6" dark red corner triangle with a 6" medium green corner triangle, placing right sides together and aligning the long edges. Make 14 pairs. Cut the corner pairs into Method One bias strips at the 2¾" mark. See page 22.
4. Sew the pairs of bias strips on their long edges and then join the pairs to make Strip Unit III. Cut 40 bias squares, each 2½" x 2½", from Strip Unit III.

Strip Unit III
Make 1

Cut 40

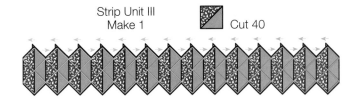

5. Repeat steps 3 and 4 with the reserved 6" dark green corner triangles and 6" medium red corner triangles to make Strip Unit IV. Cut 36 bias squares, each 2½" x 2½", from Strip Unit IV.

Strip Unit IV
Make 1

Cut 36

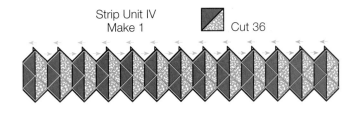

Dark green   Medium green   Dark red   Medium red   Background

6. Sew a dark red/medium green bias square to the left side of a dark green/medium red bias square. Make 16 pairs.

Make 16

7. Join 4 pairs from step 6 to make a left half row.

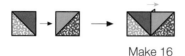

Make 4 left half rows.

8. Sew a dark green/medium red bias square to the left side of a dark red/ medium green bias square.

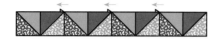

Make 16

9. Join 4 pairs from step 8 to make a right half row.

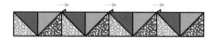

Make 4 right half rows.

10. Re-press the seams of 4 of the 8 remaining dark red/ medium green bias squares toward the medium green. Sew a bias square with the seam pressed toward the medium green to a bias square with the seam pressed toward the dark red to make a row center.

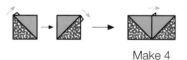

Make 4

11. Sew a left half row and a right half row to opposite sides of a row center to make a pieced border strip.

Left half row   Right half row

Make 4 border strips.

12. Following the directions on page 95 for "Pieced Borders," measure the pieced borders to see if they are the same size as the quilt sides. It may be necessary to take in or let out some of the seams between the bias squares to fit the borders to the edges of the quilt. Sew 2 of the pieced border strips to opposite sides of the quilt top, with the medium and dark red triangles toward the center of the quilt. Press seams toward the inner border.

13. Sew a dark green/medium red bias square to each end of the remaining pieced border strips. Press seams toward the outside bias squares. Sew these pieced border strips to the top and bottom edges of the quilt top. Press seams toward the inner border.

14. Refer to the general directions for quilt finishing, beginning on page 95. Layer the completed quilt top with batting and backing; baste. Quilt as desired. Bind the edges of the quilt. Label the quilt.

Dark green   Medium green   Dark red   Medium red   Background

Pinwheel Shadow

Color photo on page 28.

Finished Quilt Size
44" x 52"

Finished Block Size
8" x 8"

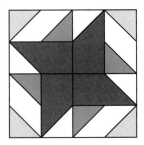

Pinwheel Shadow

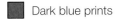 Dark blue prints

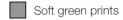 Soft green prints

Rust prints

Tan print

Materials: 44"-wide fabric

$\frac{1}{8}$ yd. each of 9 dark blue prints
11" x 18" piece each of 8 soft green prints
11" x 18" piece each of 8 rust prints
$1\frac{1}{4}$ yds. tan print
$\frac{3}{8}$ yd. rust print for inner border
$\frac{3}{4}$ yd. dark multicolor print for outer border
$\frac{3}{8}$ yd. binding
$3\frac{3}{8}$ yds. backing

CUTTING

All measurements include ¼"-wide seam allowances.

From *each* of the dark blue prints, cut:
1 strip, 2½" x 42"; crosscut into:
    9 rectangles, each 2½" x 4½", for block
      piecing

From *each* of the soft green and rust prints, cut:
1 piece, 9" x 16", for Strip Unit I

From the rust border print, cut:
4 strips, each 2¼" x 42", for inner border

From the dark multicolor print, cut:
5 strips, each 4½" x 42", for outer border

From the tan print, cut:
2 pieces, each 9" x 42", for Strip Unit I
1 piece, 9" x 42"; crosscut into:
    1 piece, 9" x 20", for Strip Unit I
    24 squares, each 2½" x 2½", for block
      piecing
4 strips, each 2½" x 42"; crosscut into:
    56 squares, each 2½" x 2½", for block
      piecing

From the fabric for binding, cut:
5 strips, each 2" x 42"

Refer to the instructions on page 19 for cutting Method Two bias strips.

Using the Bias Stripper, cut the number and size of full bias strips indicated in the chart. Cut all fabrics face down. If you are left-handed, cut all fabrics face up. Set aside the leftover corner triangles for a pieced backing or another project.

FABRIC	NO. OF PIECES	SIZE	CUTTING MARK	TOTAL NO. FULL BIAS STRIPS
Soft greens	8	**9" x 16"**	2¾"	**16**
Rust prints	8	**9" x 16"**	2¾"	**16**
Tan	2	**9" x 42"**	2"	**28**
	1	**9" x 20"**		

PIECING THE BLOCKS

Refer to the instructions on pages 19–21 for making striped rectangles. Press seam allowances in the direction of the arrows unless otherwise instructed.

1. Assemble 4 Strip Unit I. Randomly choose 4 soft green, 4 rust, and 7 tan bias strips for each strip unit. Cut a total of 80 striped rectangles, each 2½" x 4½", from Strip Unit I.

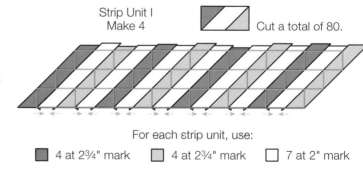

Strip Unit I
Make 4

Cut a total of 80.

For each strip unit, use:

☐ 4 at 2¾" mark   ☐ 4 at 2¾" mark   ☐ 7 at 2" mark

■ Dark blue   ■ Soft green   □ Rust   □ Tan

2. On the wrong side of each of the 80 tan 2½" squares, draw a line from corner to corner. Use a fine-line mechanical pencil and a sandpaper board to keep the fabric from shifting while marking. See page 6 for making a sandpaper board.

3. With right sides together, place a tan square on one end of a dark blue rectangle. Stitch on the pencil line. Cut away the excess corner fabric ¼" from the stitching line. Press the seam toward the tan triangle.

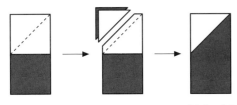

Make 80

4. Sew a blue/tan pieced rectangle to a striped rectangle, butting the diagonal seams at the corner.

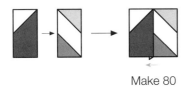

Make 80

5. Sew the rectangle pairs together to make 40 half blocks.

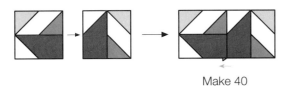

Make 40

6. Sew 2 half blocks together to complete a Pinwheel Shadow block. Make 20 blocks.

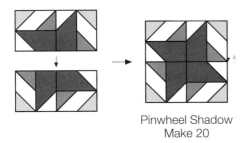

Pinwheel Shadow
Make 20

ASSEMBLING AND FINISHING THE QUILT TOP

1. Lay out the blocks in a pleasing color arrangement. Make 5 rows of 4 blocks each. Alternate the direction of the final block seam from block to block in each row so that the seams butt when joining the rows.

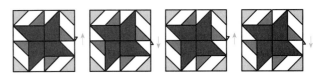

2. Sew the blocks together in horizontal rows. Press seams in alternate directions from row to row. Join the rows; press seams in either direction.
3. Attach the 2¼"-wide rust inner border to the quilt top, following the directions for "Plain Borders" on page 95. Repeat for the 4½"-wide dark multicolor outer border.
4. Refer to the general directions for quilt finishing, beginning on page 95. Layer the completed quilt top with batting and backing; baste. Quilt as desired. Bind the edges of the quilt. Label the quilt.

 Dark blue   Soft green   Rust   Tan

COLOR PHOTO ON
PAGE 26.

FINISHED QUILT SIZE
53½" x 53½"

FINISHED BLOCK SIZE
9" x 9"

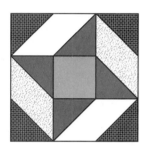

Block A

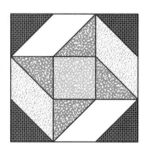

Block B

 Black print

Dark blue print

Medium blue print

Light blue print

Dark gold print

Medium gold print

Light gold print

MATERIALS: 44"-WIDE FABRIC

1¾ yds. black multicolor print (includes border)
⅞ yd. dark blue print
¼ yd. medium blue print
1⅛ yds. light blue print
⅞ yd. dark gold print
¼ yd. medium gold print
1⅛ yds. light gold print
⅜ yd. binding
3½ yds. backing

CUTTING

All measurements include ¼"-wide seam allowances.

From the black multicolor print, cut:
3 pieces, each 12" x 42", for Strip Units I, II, III, and IV
5 strips, each 4½" x 42", for outer border

From the dark blue print, cut:
2 pieces, each 12" x 42", for Strip Units I and II

From the medium blue print, cut:
1 strip, 3½" x 42"; crosscut into:
    12 squares, each 3½" x 3½", for Block A piecing.
    Cut a 13th square from leftover fabric.

From the light blue print, cut:
3 pieces, each 12" x 42", for Strip Units II and III

From the dark gold print, cut:
2 pieces, each 12" x 42", for Strip Units III and IV

From the medium gold print, cut:
1 strip, 3½" x 42"; crosscut into:
    12 squares, each 3½" x 3½", for Block B piecing

From the light gold print, cut:
3 pieces, each 12" x 42", for Strip Units I and IV

From the fabric for binding, cut:
6 strips, each 2" x 42"

Refer to the instructions on page 19 for cutting Method Two bias strips.

Using the Bias Stripper, cut the 12" x 42" fabric pieces into the number and sizes of full-size bias strips indicated in the chart. Cut all fabrics face down. If you are left-handed, cut all fabrics face up. Set aside the leftover corner triangles for a pieced backing or another project.

FABRIC	NO. OF 12" x 42" PIECES	CUTTING MARK	TOTAL NO. FULL BIAS STRIPS	STRIP UNIT
Black multi	3	3¾"	19	**I, II, III, IV**
Dark blue	2	3¾"	10	**I, II**
Light blue	3	3"	17	**II, III**
Dark gold	2	3¾"	9	**III, IV**
Light gold	3	3"	17	**I, IV**

PIECING THE BLOCKS

Refer to the instructions on pages 19–21 for making striped rectangles. Press seam allowances in the direction of the arrows unless otherwise instructed.

1. Assemble 1 Strip Unit I. Cut 26 striped rectangles, each 3½" x 6½", from Strip Unit I.

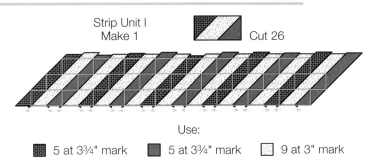

Strip Unit I
Make 1

Cut 26

Use:

 5 at 3¾" mark   5 at 3¾" mark   9 at 3" mark

Black   Dark blue   Medium blue   Light blue   Dark gold   Medium gold   Light gold

2. Assemble 1 Strip Unit II. Cut 26 striped rectangles, each 3½" x 6½", from Strip Unit II.

Strip Unit II
Make 1

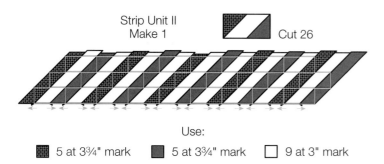

Cut 26

Use:

■ 5 at 3¾" mark ■ 5 at 3¾" mark ☐ 9 at 3" mark

3. Assemble 1 Strip Unit III. Cut 24 striped rectangles, each 3½" x 6½", from Strip Unit III.

Strip Unit III
Make 1

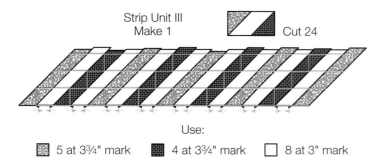

Cut 24

Use:

▨ 5 at 3¾" mark ▨ 4 at 3¾" mark ☐ 8 at 3" mark

4. Assemble 1 Strip Unit IV. Cut 24 striped rectangles, each 3½" x 6½", from Strip Unit IV.

Strip Unit IV
Make 1

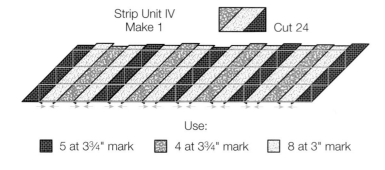

Cut 24

Use:

■ 5 at 3¾" mark ▨ 4 at 3¾" mark ☐ 8 at 3" mark

5. For Block A, sew a striped rectangle from Strip Unit II to the top of a 3½" medium blue square. Stitch from the corner of the square to the halfway point, stop, and remove the unit from the machine. This is called a half seam.

6. Sew a striped rectangle from Strip Unit I to the right side of the unit from step 5, stitching from edge to edge.

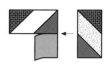

7. Sew a striped rectangle from Strip Unit II to the bottom of the unit, stitching from edge to edge.

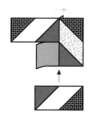

8. Sew a striped rectangle from Strip Unit I to the left side of the unit, stitching from edge to edge. Stitch the remainder of the half seam to complete Block A.

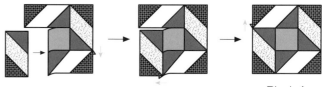

Block A
Make 13

 Black   Dark blue   Medium blue ☐ Light blue   Dark gold   Medium gold   Light gold

9. For Block B, sew a striped rectangle from Strip Unit III to the top of a 3½" medium gold square, using a half seam as described in step 5.

10. Sew a striped rectangle from Strip Unit IV to the right side of the unit, stitching from edge to edge.

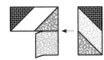

11. Sew a striped rectangle from Strip Unit III to the bottom of the unit, stitching from edge to edge.

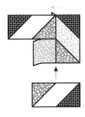

12. Sew a striped rectangle from Strip Unit IV to the left side of the unit, stitching from edge to edge. Stitch the remainder of the half seam to complete Block B.

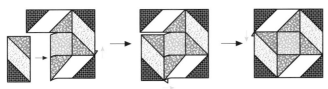

Block B
Make 12

ASSEMBLING AND FINISHING THE QUILT TOP

1. Lay out the blocks as shown. Sew the blocks together in 5 horizontal rows of 5 blocks each. Press seams in opposite directions from row to row.

2. Join the rows; press seams in either direction.
3. Attach the 4½"-wide black print border to the quilt top, following the directions for "Plain Borders" on page 95. Press seams toward the border.
4. Refer to the general directions for quilt finishing, beginning on page 95. Layer the completed quilt top with batting and backing; baste. Quilt as desired. Bind the edges of the quilt. Label the quilt.

 Black Dark blue Medium blue Light blue Dark gold Medium gold Light gold

RADIANCE

COLOR PHOTO ON PAGE 26.

FINISHED QUILT SIZE
66½" x 66½"

FINISHED BLOCK SIZE
12" x 12"

Block A

Block B

 Dark prints

 Medium prints

 Light prints

Make this quilt as large or as small as you wish. Block fabric requirements are given for trios of prints that make two complete blocks per trio. The sample quilt has sixteen blocks and therefore eight fabric trios. Border, backing, and binding fabric requirements are for the sixteen-block version shown on page 26. All of us who made this quilt found it best to wait until after the blocks were sewn together before selecting the border fabrics.

MATERIALS: 44"-WIDE FABRIC

For every 2 blocks, you need:
³⁄₈ yd. or 1 fat quarter* of a dark print
³⁄₈ yd. or 1 fat quarter* of a medium print
³⁄₈ yd. light print
*Please note that a fat quarter must measure no less than 17" x 21"
after washing or it will not be adequate in size.

Borders and Finishing

³⁄₈ yd. for inner border	1½ yds. for outer	½ yd. for binding
⁵⁄₈ yd. for middle border	border	4¼ yds. for backing

CUTTING

All measurements include ¼"-wide seam allowances.
**The following cutting instructions for the dark, medium, and light prints are for making
1 Block A and 1 Block B. Repeat as necessary with each dark/medium/light combination to
make the number of blocks required for the quilt size you are making.**

From the dark print for each pair of blocks, cut:
2 pieces, each 7" x 18", for Strip Units I and II
8 squares, each 2½" x 2½", for Block A and
    Block B piecing

From the medium print for each pair of blocks, cut:
2 pieces, each 7" x 14", for Strip Units I and II
1 square, 4½" x 4½", for Block A piecing
4 squares, each 2½" x 2½", for Block B piecing

From the light print for each pair of blocks, cut:
2 pieces, each 7" x 18", for Strip Units I and II
1 square, 4½" x 4½", for Block B piecing
4 squares, each 2½" x 2½", for Block A piecing

From the fabric for inner border, cut:
5 strips, each 1½" x 42"

From the fabric for middle border, cut:
6 strips, each 2½" x 42"

From the fabric for outer border, cut:
7 strips, each 6½" x 42"

From the fabric for binding, cut:
7 strips, each 2" x 42"

Bias Strip Cutting Chart for 2 Blocks

Refer to the instructions on page 19 for cutting Method Two bias strips.

Using the Bias Stripper, cut the number and size of full bias strips indicated in the chart. Pay attention to the fabric direction when cutting. If you are left-handed, cut all fabric in the opposite direction from that stated in the chart. Reserve the 7" leftover corner triangles for use later in the quilt.

FABRIC	SIZE	FABRIC DIRECTION	CUTTING MARK	TOTAL NO. FULL BIAS STRIPS	STRIP UNIT
Dark	7" x 18"	face up	2"	4	I
Dark	7" x 18"	face down	2"	4	II
Medium	7" x 14"	face up	2¾"	2	I
Medium	7" x 14"	face down	2¾"	2	II
Light	7" x 18"	face up	2¾"	3	I
Light	7" x 18"	face down	2¾"	3	II

PIECING THE BLOCKS

Refer to the instructions on pages 19–21 for making striped rectangles, and page 22 for reusing Method Two corner triangles. Press seam allowances in the direction of the arrows unless otherwise instructed.

1. Assemble 1 Strip Unit I. Cut 8 striped rectangles, each 2½" x 4½", from Strip Unit I.

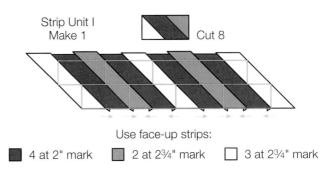

Strip Unit I
Make 1

Cut 8

Use face-up strips:

■ Dark — 4 at 2" mark   ■ Medium — 2 at 2¾" mark   □ Light — 3 at 2¾" mark

 Dark   Medium   Light

2. Assemble 1 Strip Unit II. Cut 8 striped rectangles, each 2½" x 4½", from Strip Unit II.

Strip Unit II
Make 1

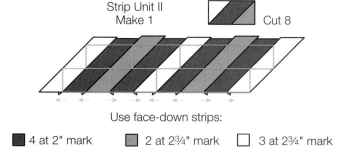

Cut 8

Use face-down strips:

■ 4 at 2" mark   ■ 2 at 2¾" mark   □ 3 at 2¾" mark

3. Pair the 4 dark 7" corner triangles with 2 of the medium and 2 of the light 7" corner triangles, placing right sides together and aligning the long edges. You should have 2 dark/medium pairs and 2 dark/light pairs. Cut the corner pairs into Method One bias strips at the 2¾" mark. See page 22. Save the remaining pairs of small triangles left over after cutting bias strips for step 5.

4. Sew the bias strip pairs together on the long edges. Join the pairs to make Strip Unit III. Cut 11 bias squares, each 2½" x 2½", from Strip Unit III. Save the edge triangles for step 5.

Strip Unit III

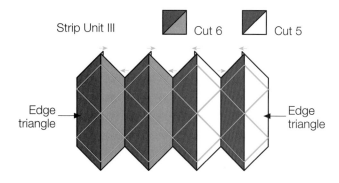

Cut 6   Cut 5

Edge triangle   Edge triangle

5. Sew the pairs of small triangles left over from step 3 on the long edges. You should have 2 dark/medium pairs and 2 dark/light pairs. Nub and resize the dark and light edge triangles left over from step 4. See page 10. Sew them right sides together on the long edge. You should now have 2 dark/medium units and 3 dark/light units. Cut these units into 2½" bias

squares for a total of 8 dark/medium and 8 dark/light bias squares from steps 4 and 5.

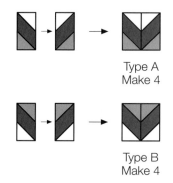

Make 2 dark/medium.   Make 2 dark/light.   Make 1 dark/light from nubbed edge triangles.

6. Sew the 16 striped rectangles into 2 types of pairs: 4 Type A and 4 Type B. Press seams open.

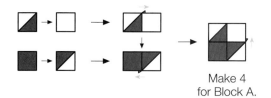

Type A
Make 4

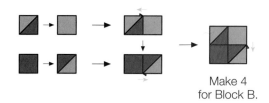

Type B
Make 4

7. Assemble 4 Block A corner units.

Make 4
for Block A.

8. Assemble 4 Block B corner units.

Make 4
for Block B.

9. Sew a Block A corner unit to opposite sides of a Type A rectangle pair. Make 2. Sew a Block B corner unit to opposite sides of a Type B rectangle pair. Make 2.

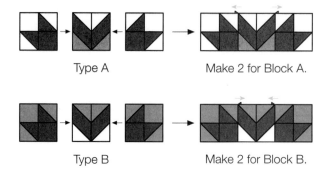

Type A   Make 2 for Block A.

Type B   Make 2 for Block B.

■ Dark   ■ Medium   □ Light

10. Sew the remaining 2 Type A rectangle pairs to opposite sides of the medium 4½" square. Sew the remaining 2 Type B rectangle pairs to opposite sides of the light 4½" square.

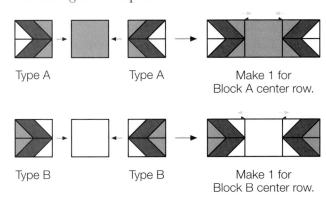

Type A   Type A   Make 1 for
                            Block A center row.

Type B   Type B   Make 1 for
                            Block B center row.

11. Make 1 Block A by sewing the 2 Block A rows from step 9 to opposite sides of the Block A center row.

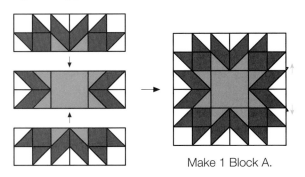

Make 1 Block A.

12. Make 1 Block B by sewing the 2 Block B rows from step 9 to opposite sides of the Block B center row.

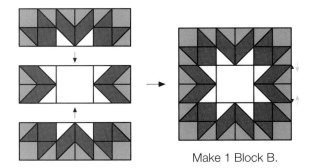

Make 1 Block B.

13. Follow the same procedure to make as many pairs of blocks as needed for your quilt. The sample quilt requires a total of 16 blocks (8 pairs of blocks).

ASSEMBLING AND FINISHING THE QUILT TOP

1. Lay out the blocks in a pleasing arrangement, alternating Block A and Block B. Make 4 rows of 4 blocks each. Sew the blocks together in horizontal rows. Press seams in opposite directions from row to row.

2. Join the rows; press seams in either direction.
3. Attach the 1½"-wide inner border to the quilt top, following the directions for "Plain Borders" on page 95. Repeat for the 2½"-wide middle and 6½"-wide outer borders.
4. Refer to the general directions for quilt finishing, beginning on page 95. Layer the completed quilt top with batting and backing; baste. Quilt as desired. Bind the edges of the quilt. Label the quilt.

■ Dark   ■ Medium   □ Light

JACK FROST

COLOR PHOTO ON
PAGE 53.

FINISHED QUILT SIZE
71¼" x 71¼"

FINISHED BLOCK SIZE
10" x 10"

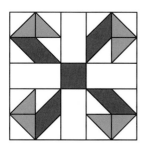

Jack-in-the-Box

■ Darks

■ Mediums

□ Background

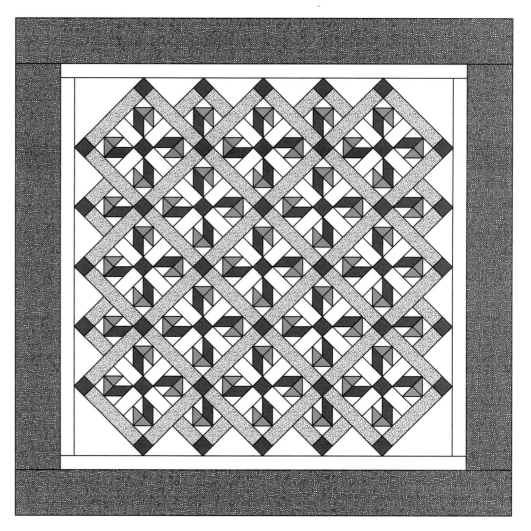

This is another quilt where the thirteen blocks are made in pairs (seven pairs with one leftover block). In addition, you need an eighth pair of uncompleted blocks for the pieced side setting triangles. I chose eight pairs of dark/medium combinations and one background fabric for all the blocks.

MATERIALS: 44"-WIDE FABRIC

1 piece, 10" x 21", each of 8 dark prints and 8 medium prints
3 yds. background (includes side triangles and inner border)
1 yd. fabric for sashing
1½ yds. fabric for outer border
½ yd. binding
4½ yds. backing

CUTTING

All measurements include ¼"-wide seam allowances.

From *each* of the 8 dark prints, cut:
1 piece, 6" x 17", for Strip Unit I
2 squares, each 2½" x 2½", for block centers (do not cut these for the 8th pair)
4 squares, each 2½" x 2½", for sashing squares

From *each* of the 8 medium prints, cut:
1 piece, 6" x 20", for Strip Unit II

From the fabric for sashing, cut:
11 strips, each 2½" x 42"; crosscut into:
  36 strips, each 2½" x 10½", for sashings
  16 rectangles, each 2½" x 4½", for side triangles

From the fabric for outer border, cut:
7 strips, each 7" x 42"

From the background print, cut:
8 pieces, each 6" x 42", for Strip Units I and II
7 strips, each 2½" x 42"; crosscut into:
  56 rectangles, each 2½" x 4½", for block piecing
1 strip, 10¼" x 42"; crosscut into:
  4 squares, each 10¼" x 10¼", for side triangles
1 strip, 11¼" x 42"; crosscut into:
  2 squares, each 11¼" x 11¼", for corner triangles
6 strips, each 2½" x 42", for inner border

From the fabric for binding, cut:
7 strips, each 2" x 42"

The following chart contains cutting instructions to make 2 Jack-in-the-Box blocks from one dark/medium combination. Repeat with 6 dark/medium combinations to make 12 more blocks for a total of 14.

Refer to the instructions on page 19 for cutting Method Two bias strips.

Using the Bias Stripper, cut the number and size of full bias strips indicated in the chart. Cut all fabrics face up. If you are left-handed, cut all fabrics face down. Reserve 1 medium and 1 light leftover 6" corner triangle for Strip Unit II. Set aside the remaining dark, medium, and light corner triangles for a pieced backing or another project.

FABRIC	SIZE	CUTTING MARK	TOTAL NO. FULL BIAS STRIPS	STRIP UNIT
Darks	6" x 17"	2"	4	I
Mediums	6" x 20"	2¾"	4	II
Background	6" x 42"	2¾"	9	I & II

PIECING THE BLOCKS

Refer to the instructions on pages 19–22 for making striped rectangles and bias squares. Press all seams in the direction of the arrows unless otherwise instructed.

To make 2 blocks:
1. Assemble 1 Strip Unit I. Cut 8 striped rectangles, each 2½" x 4½", from Strip Unit I.

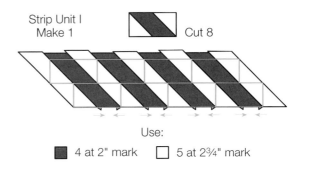

Strip Unit I
Make 1

Cut 8

Use:
■ 4 at 2" mark □ 5 at 2¾" mark

■ Darks ■ Mediums □ Background

2. Assemble 1 Strip Unit II. Sew the reserved light and medium corner triangles to opposite sides of the strip unit. Cut 16 bias squares, each 2½" x 2½", from Strip Unit II. You should have 8 bias squares pressed toward the light and 8 pressed toward the medium.

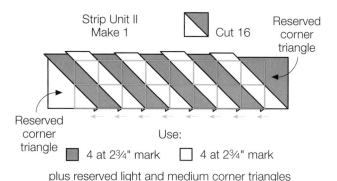

Strip Unit II
Make 1

Cut 16

Reserved corner triangle

Reserved corner triangle

Use:

■ 4 at 2¾" mark □ 4 at 2¾" mark

plus reserved light and medium corner triangles

3. Sew the bias squares into pairs, using 1 bias square pressed toward the light and 1 bias square pressed toward the medium in each pair.

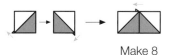

Make 8

4. Sew a bias-square pair to each striped rectangle.

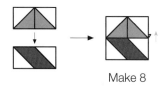

Make 8

5. Sew a unit made in step 4 to opposite sides of a 2½" x 4½" background rectangle to make an outer row.

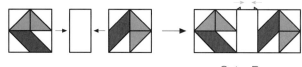

Outer Row
Make 4

6. Sew a 2½" x 4½" background rectangle to opposite sides of a 2½" dark square to make a center row.

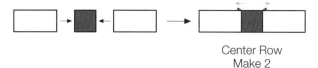

Center Row
Make 2

7. Sew an outer row to opposite sides of a center row to complete a Jack-in-the-Box block.

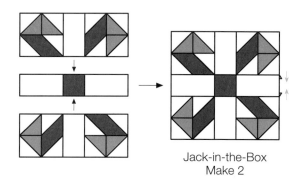

Jack-in-the-Box
Make 2

8. Using the other 6 dark/medium fabric pairs and background pieces, make 12 more blocks for a total of 14 blocks. Choose your 13 favorites and set aside one for the backing, a pillow, or a sampler block collection.

ASSEMBLING AND FINISHING THE QUILT TOP

1. Using the 8th dark/medium fabric pair and the remaining 6" x 42" background piece, cut bias strips as in the chart. Follow steps 1–4 under "Piecing the Blocks" to make 8 partial block units.

Make 8 partial blocks.

2. Sew a partial block unit to a 2½" x 4½" sashing strip.

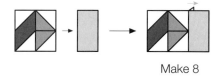

Make 8

3. Sew a sashing rectangle to a 2½" sashing square. Sew each unit to a unit made in step 2.

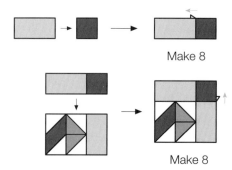

Make 8

Make 8

4. Cut the 10¼" background squares once diagonally to yield 16 side triangles.

■ Darks ■ Mediums □ Background

5. Sew a side triangle to the top of each unit made in step 3. Add a second triangle to the adjacent side.

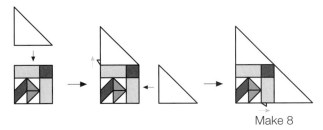

Make 8

6. Lay out the blocks, pieced side triangles, the 2½" x 10½" sashing strips, and the dark 2½" sashing squares as shown. Arrange and balance the different blocks and assorted sashing squares in a pleasing arrangement.

Row A   Row B

Center Row

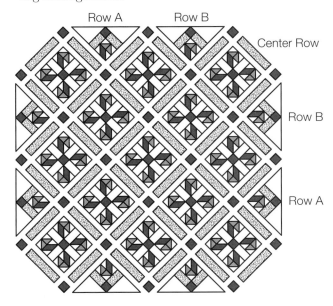

Row B

Row A

7. To make Row A, sew a 2½" x 10½" sashing strip to opposite sides of the block. Sew a 2½" sashing square to each end of a third sashing strip and sew this unit to the top of the block. Add a pieced side triangle to opposite sides of the block. Make 2 Row A.

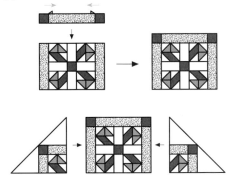

8. To make Row B, sew the 3 blocks and 4 sashing strips together. Sew the 3 sashing strips and 4 dark 2½" sashing squares together. Join the pieced sashing

strip to the top of the row of blocks. Add a pieced side triangle to each end of the row. Make 2 Row B.

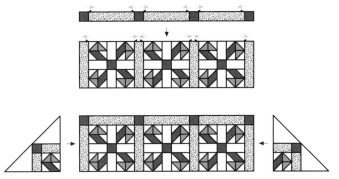

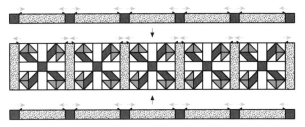

9. To make the center row, sew the 5 blocks and 6 sashing strips together. Sew the 5 sashing strips and 6 dark 2½" sashing squares together. Join the pieced sashing strips to opposite sides of the row of blocks.

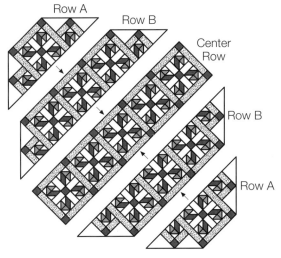

10. Sew Rows A and B to either side of the center row to complete the center of the quilt top.

Row A

Row B

Center Row

Row B

Row A

11. Cut the 11¼" background squares twice diagonally to yield 4 corner triangles. Sew these to the 4 corners of the quilt top.

12. Attach the 2½"-wide inner border to the quilt top, following the directions for "Plain Borders" on page 95. Repeat for the 7"-wide outer border.

13. Refer to the general directions for quilt finishing, beginning on page 95. Layer the completed quilt top with batting and backing; baste. Quilt as desired. Bind the edges of the quilt. Label the quilt.

■ Darks   ▦ Mediums   ☐ Background

SNOWFLAKE MAGIC

COLOR PHOTO ON
PAGE 54.

FINISHED QUILT SIZE
82½" x 82½"

FINISHED BLOCK SIZE
12" x 12"

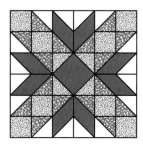

Block A

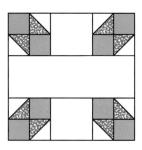

Block B

■ Dark purple print

▨ Light purple print

▨ Pink print

▨ Green print

□ Light print

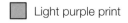

MATERIALS: 44"-WIDE FABRIC

2¾ yds. dark purple print (includes outer border)
⅝ yd. light purple print
2⅛ yds. green print (includes middle border)
⅞ yd. pink print
3⅛ yds. light print (includes inner border)
⅝ yd. binding
7½ yds. backing

CUTTING

All measurements include ¼"-wide seam allowances.

From the dark purple print, cut:
2 pieces, each 12" x 42", for Strip Units I and II
1 piece, 12" x 42"; crosscut into:
    2 pieces, each 12" x 21", for Strip Units I and II
1 strip, 4½" x 42"; crosscut into:
    9 squares, each 4½" x 4½", for Block A
        piecing*
8 strips, each 6½" x 42", for outer border
*You will need to cut 4 additional squares from
    leftovers.

From the green print, cut:
3 pieces, each 12" x 42", for Strip Units I, II, and III
1 piece, 12" x 42"; crosscut into:
    1 piece, 12" x 21", for Strip Unit III
    1 square, 12" x 12", for Strip Unit IV
8 strips, each 2½" x 42", for middle border

From the pink print, cut:
10 strips, each 2½" x 42"; crosscut into:
    156 squares, each 2½" x 2½", for Block A piecing

From the light purple print, cut:
6 strips, each 2½" x 42"; crosscut into:
    96 squares, each 2½" x 2½", for Block B
        piecing

From the light print, cut:
3 pieces, each 12" x 42", for Strip Units I, II, and III
1 piece, 12" x 42"; crosscut into:
    1 piece, 12" x 21", for Strip Unit III
    1 square, 12" x 12", for Strip Unit IV
7 strips, each 4½" x 42"; crosscut into:
    12 bars, each 4½" x 12½", for Block B
        piecing
    24 squares, each 4½" x 4½", for Block B
        piecing
8 strips, each 3½" x 42", for inner border

From the fabric for binding, cut:
8 strips, each 2" x 42"

Bias Strip Cutting Chart

Refer to the instructions on page 19 for cutting Method Two bias strips.

Using the Bias Stripper, cut the number and size of full bias strips indicated in the chart. Pay attention to the fabric direction when cutting. If you are left-handed, cut all fabrics in the opposite direction from that stated in the chart. Reserve the 8 green and 8 light 12" corner triangles for use later in the quilt.

FABRIC	NO. OF PIECES	SIZE	FABRIC DIRECTION	CUTTING MARK	TOTAL NO. FULL BIAS STRIPS	STRIP UNIT
Dark purple	1	12" x 42"	face down	2"	11	I
	1	12" x 21"	face down	2"	3	I
	1	12" x 42"	face up	2"	11	II
	1	12" x 21"	face up	2"	3	II
Green	3	12" x 42"	face down	2¾"	24	I, III
	1	12" x 42"	face up	2¾"	8	II
Light	3	12" x 42"	face down	2¾"	24	I, III
	1	12" x 42"	face up	2¾"	8	II

Cut 4 additional 4½" squares from the leftover dark purple corner triangles and set these aside for Block A piecing. Set aside the others for a pieced backing or another project.

Dark purple   Light purple   Pink   Green   Light

Piecing the Blocks

Refer to the instructions on pages 19–21 for making striped rectangles, and pages 17–22 for making Method One and Method Two bias squares. Press seam allowances in the direction of the arrows unless otherwise instructed.

1. Assemble 2 Strip Unit I. Cut a total of 52 striped rectangles, each 2½" x 4½", from Strip Unit I.

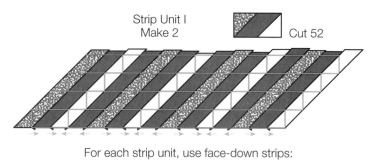

Strip Unit I
Make 2
Cut 52

For each strip unit, use face-down strips:
■ 7 at 2" mark ▨ 4 at 2¾" mark □ 4 at 2¾" mark

2. Assemble 2 Strip Unit II. Cut a total of 52 striped rectangles, each 2½" x 4½", from Strip Unit II.

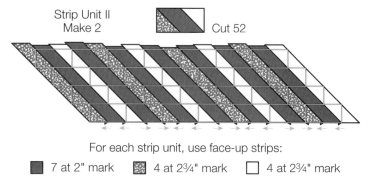

Strip Unit II
Make 2
Cut 52

For each strip unit, use face-up strips:
■ 7 at 2" mark ▨ 4 at 2¾" mark □ 4 at 2¾" mark

3. Cut 2 of the green and 2 of the light print 12" corner triangles into Method One bias strips at the 2¾" mark. See page 22.

4. Assemble 2 Strip Unit III. Cut a total of 140 bias squares, each 2½" x 2½", from Strip Unit III.

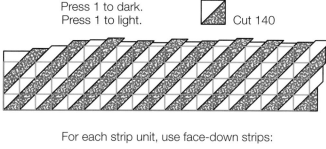

Strip Unit III
Make 2
Press 1 to dark.
Press 1 to light.
Cut 140

For each strip unit, use face-down strips:
▨ 8 at 2¾" mark □ 8 at 2¾" mark
plus corner bias strips from step 3

5. Pair the remaining 6 green and 6 light print 12" corner triangles, placing right sides together and aligning the long edges. Cut the corner triangles into Method One bias strips at the 2¾" mark. See page 22. You will have 2 lengths of bias strips.

6. Sew the same-length pairs of bias strips on their long edges and then join the pairs to make 1 tall and 1 short Strip Unit IV. Press seams in the tall unit toward the green strips and toward the light print strips in the short unit. Cut a total of 67 bias squares, each 2½" x 2½", from Strip Unit IV.

Strip Unit IV
Make 1 tall.
Cut 67

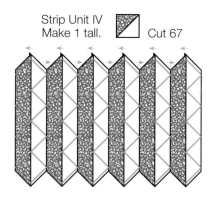

Strip Unit IV
Make 1 short.

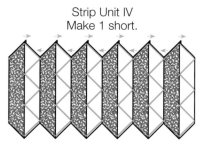

 Dark purple ▨ Light purple ▨ Pink ▨ Green □ Light

7. You should now have more than 200 green/light print bias squares. Sort them into 2 stacks, one with 104 units pressed toward the green and a second with 96 units pressed toward the light. Set aside the extra bias squares for another project.

8. Draw a diagonal line from corner to corner on the wrong side of 52 of the 2½" pink squares. Use a fine-line mechanical pencil and a sandpaper board to keep the fabric from shifting while marking. See page 6 for making a sandpaper board.

9. Place a marked pink square on one corner of a 4½" dark purple square, right sides together. Pin in place and sew on the pencil line. Fold the pink corner up over the dark purple corner to check for accuracy. Adjust and restitch if necessary. Trim away the excess fabric ¼" from the sewing line and press the seam allowance toward the pink triangle. Repeat with the remaining 3 corners of the dark purple square to make a Block A center square.

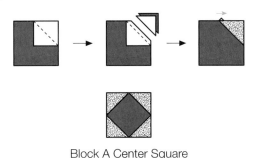

Block A Center Square
Make 13

10. Sew a left striped rectangle to a right striped rectangle, butting the diagonal seams. Press center seams open. Make 52 striped rectangle pairs.

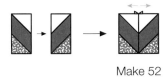

Make 52

11. Sew a green/light print bias square pressed toward the green to a 2½" pink square. Sew 2 of these units together as shown to make a Block A corner unit.

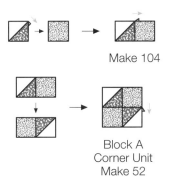

Make 104

Block A
Corner Unit
Make 52

12. Sew a Block A corner unit to opposite sides of a striped rectangle pair to make a Block A outer row.

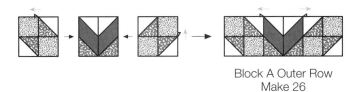

Block A Outer Row
Make 26

13. Sew a striped rectangle pair to opposite sides of a Block A center square to make a Block A center row.

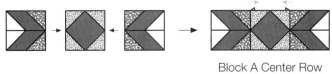

Block A Center Row
Make 13

14. Sew a Block A outer row to opposite sides of a Block A center row to complete Block A.

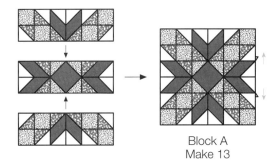

Block A
Make 13

 Dark purple   Light purple   Pink   Green   Light

15. Sew a bias square pressed toward the light to a 2½" light purple square. Sew 2 of these units together as shown to make a Block B corner unit.

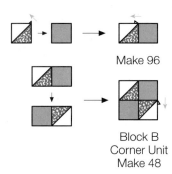

Make 96

Block B
Corner Unit
Make 48

16. Sew a Block B corner unit to opposite sides of a 4½" light print square to make a Block B outer row.

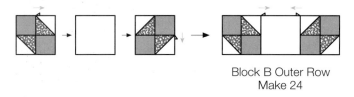

Block B Outer Row
Make 24

17. Sew a Block B outer row to opposite sides of a 4½" x 12½" light print rectangle to complete Block B.

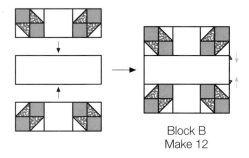

Block B
Make 12

ASSEMBLING AND FINISHING THE QUILT TOP

1. Lay out the 13 Block A and 12 Block B in 5 rows of 5 blocks each, alternating block types as shown. Sew the blocks together in horizontal rows. Press seams toward Block B.

2. Join the rows; press the seams in either direction.
3. Attach the 3½"-wide light print inner border to the quilt top, following the directions for "Plain Borders" on page 95. Repeat for the 2½"-wide green middle border and the 6½"-wide dark purple outer border.
4. Refer to the general directions for quilt finishing, beginning on page 95. Layer the completed quilt top with batting and backing; baste. Quilt as desired. Bind the edges of the quilt. Label the quilt.

 Dark purple Light purple Pink Green Light

Jack Frost
by Donna Lynn Thomas, 1994, Lansing, Kansas, 71¼" x 71¼".

The cool, icy blue and turquoise are warmed slightly by the touches of pink in the background print of this frosty quilt. Quilted icicles slash across the quilt in many shades of blue, green, and silver metallic threads—brrrrr. Machine quilted by Kari Lane. Directions begin on page 44.

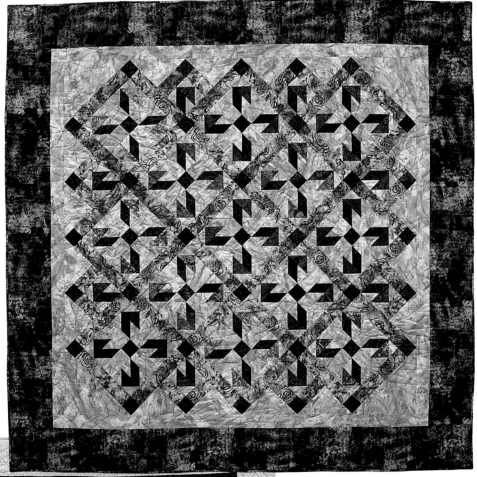

Ribbons and Bows
by M. Deborah Rose, 1994, Ft. Leavenworth, Kansas, 71¼" x 71¼".

Deb took the time to do some special things to her quilt. Notice the varied but careful placement of background fabrics in the blocks and quilt top. She used a pretty floral print for the inner sashings and a complementary floral border print for the outer sashings. The result is a delightfully feminine quilt, enhanced by the beautiful hand quilting. Hand quilted by Aline Duerr and Norma Jean Rohman.

Snowflake Magic
by Mildred Gerdes,
1994, Lansing, Kansas,
82½" x 82½".

*Mildred carried out the
snowflake theme to perfection.
The delicate snowflake print
used as the background is perfect
with the deep royal purple, clear
pink, and cool turquoise prints
in the piecing. Beautifully hand
quilted, Mildred's quilt is a rich
feast for the eyes. Directions
begin on page 48.*

Stripple Star
by Donna Lynn Thomas,
1994, Lansing, Kansas,
51½" x 62¾".

*Thanks to Sally Schneider's
painless-border concept, the two
pieced borders on this quilt are
assembled right along with the
rest of the quilt in diagonal rows.
It couldn't be easier to make.
Machine quilted by Kari Lane.
Directions begin on page 61.*

Carnival!
by Kari Lane,
1994, Lansing, Kansas,
57" x 68⅜".

Kari generates excitement whenever she gets to work. She used her collection of batiks to full advantage in this lively, dancing quilt. To complete the festive theme, she machine quilted unfurled, confetti ribbons all over in a multitude of brightly hued, metallic, and ribbon threads. Directions begin on page 57.

The back of the quilt sings, too. Kari used leftovers from the quilt top to add excitement to the quilt back.

Mountain Fire
**by Donna Lynn Thomas,
1994, Lansing, Kansas,
72½" x 72½".**

I was playing with this variation of Delectable Mountains while watching reports of the 1993 fires raging through Southern California, all the while worrying about my sister, Joanne, who lives there. The use of reds, oranges, and blacks evokes the feeling of flames shimmering in the heat and ash. Quilted fingers of flame lick across the quilt with stunning effect. Machine quilted by Kari Lane.

Directions begin on page 67.

Mountain Sunset
**by Linda Kittle,
1995, Leavenworth,
Kansas,
72½" x 72½".**

Known for her sense of style and artistry with a needle, Linda outdid herself on this beautiful quilt. It must run in the family since all the fabrics were chosen by her fourteen-year-old son, Zachary. The colors truly represent the beautiful sunsets over the rolling hills of eastern Kansas. Her exquisite hand quilting makes this a true masterpiece.

CARNIVAL!

COLOR PHOTO
ON PAGE 55.

FINISHED QUILT SIZE
56⅝" x 67⅞"

FINISHED BLOCK SIZE
8" x 8"

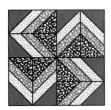

Block A

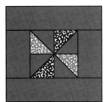

Block B

Block C

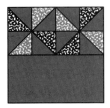

Block D

 Dark prints

Medium prints

Light prints

Black print

What makes this quilt so exciting is the gradation of color and the pieced border. To begin, select six color families. Then choose a dark, medium, and light print within each color family. Each color family will make two Block A and seven pinwheel units for Blocks B, C, and D. The pieced border is assembled at the same time as the blocks, using Sally Schneider's "painless borders" concept. You will also note that Kari used an assortment of black prints for her background fabric. The pattern instructions call for one print, but you may substitute a variety of prints as Kari did.

Materials: 44"-wide fabric

¼ yd. or 1 fat quarter each of 6 dark prints
¼ yd. or 1 fat quarter each of 6 medium prints
¼ yd. or 1 fat quarter each of 6 light prints
3⅞ yds. black print (or an assortment of black prints)
½ yd. binding
4⅜ yds. backing

Cutting

All measurements include ¼"-wide seam allowances.

From *each* of the 6 dark, 6 medium, and 6 light prints, cut:
2 pieces, each 7" x 14", for Strip Units I and II

From the black print, cut:
8 strips, each 7" x 42"; crosscut into:
    12 pieces, each 7" x 18", for Strip Units I and II
    12 squares, each 7" x 7", for Strip Unit III
    12 rectangles, each 2½" x 4½", for Block B piecing
4 strips, each 4½" x 42"; crosscut into:
    4 rectangles, each 4½" x 8½", for Block D piecing
    28 squares, each 4½" x 4½", for Block C piecing

(black print, continued):
4 strips, each 8½" x 42"; crosscut into:
    14 squares, each 8½" x 8½", for plain blocks
    12 strips, each 2½" x 8½", for Block B piecing
2 strips, each 13¼" x 42"; crosscut into:
    5 squares, each 13¼" x 13¼", for side and
      corner triangles

From the fabric for binding, cut:
7 strips, each 2" x 42"

The following chart contains cutting instructions to make 2 of Block A from one set of a dark/medium/light combination. Repeat with 5 remaining dark/medium/light combinations to make 10 more blocks for a total of 12.

Bias Strip Cutting Chart for 2 Blocks

Refer to the instructions on page 19 for cutting Method Two bias strips.

Using the Bias Stripper, cut the number and size of full bias strips indicated in the chart. Pay attention to fabric direction when cutting. Reserve the 4 dark, 4 medium, and 4 black 7" corner triangles for use later in the quilt. Set aside the 4 light 7" corner triangles for a pieced backing or another project.

FABRIC	SIZE	FABRIC DIRECTION	CUTTING MARK	TOTAL NO. FULL BIAS STRIPS	STRIP UNIT
Dark	7" x 14"	face up	2¾"	2	I
	7" x 14"	face down	2¾"	2	II
Medium	7" x 14"	face up	1"	4	I
	7" x 14"	face down	1"	4	II
Light	7" x 14"	face up	1"	4	I
	7" x 14"	face down	1"	4	II
Black	7" x 18"	face up	2¾"	3	I
	7" x 18"	face down	2¾"	3	II

 Dark   Medium   Light   Black

PIECING THE BLOCKS

Refer to the instructions on pages 19–21 for making striped rectangles, and page 22 for reusing Method Two corner triangles. Press seams in the direction of the arrows unless otherwise instructed.

BLOCK A

The following instructions make 2 blocks from each set of dark, medium, and light prints.

1. Assemble 1 Strip Unit I. Cut 8 striped rectangles, each 2½" x 4½", from Strip Unit I.

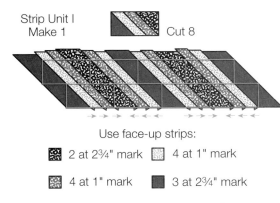

Strip Unit I
Make 1   Cut 8

Use face-up strips:

2 at 2¾" mark   4 at 1" mark

4 at 1" mark   3 at 2¾" mark

2. Assemble 1 Strip Unit II. Cut 8 striped rectangles, each 2½" x 4½", from Strip Unit II.

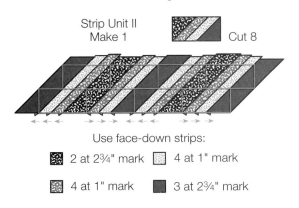

Strip Unit II
Make 1   Cut 8

Use face-down strips:

2 at 2¾" mark   4 at 1" mark

4 at 1" mark   3 at 2¾" mark

3. Sew a Strip Unit I striped rectangle to a Strip Unit II striped rectangle to make a striped rectangle pair.

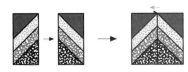

Make 8

4. Sew 2 pairs together to make half blocks.

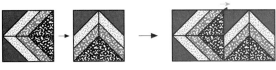

Make 4

5. Sew 2 half blocks together to complete Block A. Press the final seam in either direction.

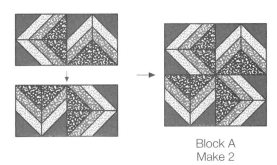

Block A
Make 2

6. Repeat steps 1–5 to make 2 Block A from each of 5 remaining sets of dark, medium, and light prints.

BLOCKS B, C, AND D

Steps 1–5 are the instructions for making 7 pinwheel units from each color family. These units are then used to make Blocks B, C, and D.

1. Cut the 12 black 7" squares once diagonally to yield 24 triangles. Combined with the 24 reserved 7" corner triangles, you should now have 48 black 7" triangles.

2. Using the 4 dark and 4 medium reserved 7" corner triangles from one color family and 8 of the black 7" triangles, pair each colored 7" triangle with a black 7" triangle, placing right sides together and aligning the long edges. Cut the triangle pairs into Method One bias strips at the 2¾" mark. See page 22.

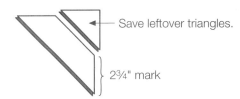

Save leftover triangles.

2¾" mark

3. Sew the pairs of bias strips together on the long edges and then sew the pairs together to make Strip Unit III. Sew the leftover corner triangle pairs from step 2 on the long edges. Cut a total of 28 bias squares, each 2½" x 2½", from Strip Unit III and the triangle pairs.

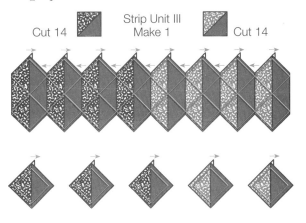

Cut 14   Strip Unit III   Cut 14
              Make 1

 Dark   Medium   Light   Black

4. Sew a dark and medium bias square together. Sew 2 of these units together to make a pinwheel.

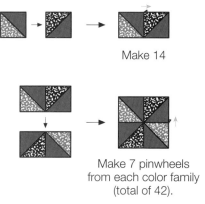

Make 14

Make 7 pinwheels
from each color family
(total of 42).

5. Repeat steps 1–4 to make 7 pinwheel units from each of the other 5 color families for a total of 42 pinwheel units.

6. Sew a 2½" x 4½" black rectangle to opposite sides of 1 pinwheel from each color family for a total of 6. Sew a 2½" x 8½" black strip to the top and bottom of each pinwheel to complete Block B.

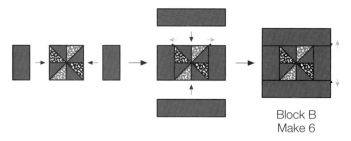

Block B
Make 6

7. Sew a black 4½" square to a pinwheel unit. Make 28 assorted pinwheel rows. Sew each row to another to complete Block C.

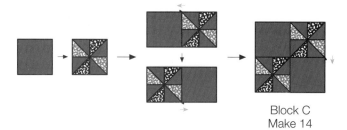

Block C
Make 14

8. Sew the remaining 8 pinwheel units into 4 pairs. Sew each pair to a black 4½" x 8½" rectangle to complete Block D.

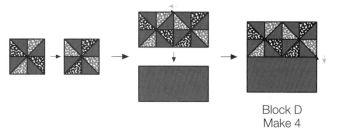

Block D
Make 4

ASSEMBLING AND FINISHING THE QUILT TOP

1. Cut the 5 black 13¼" squares twice diagonally to yield 20 quarter-square triangles. Set aside 18 triangles for the side triangles. Cut the remaining 2 triangles in half again to yield the 4 corner triangles. All of these triangles are oversized and will be trimmed to size later.

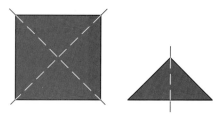

2. Lay out the A, B, C, and D blocks; the black 8½" squares; and the side triangles in diagonal rows as shown. Sew the blocks together in each row; press seams toward the black squares and side triangles.

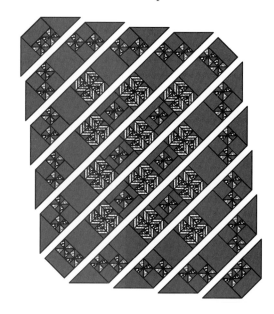

3. Join the rows; press the seams in either direction.

4. Sew the corner triangles in place; press seams toward the edges of the quilt. Trim the quilt top to ¼" from the block corners and square the quilt corners to complete the quilt top. See page 95 for trimming the quilt top.

5. Refer to the general directions for quilt finishing, beginning on page 95. Layer the completed quilt top with batting and backing; baste. Quilt as desired. Bind the edges of the quilt. Label the quilt.

 Dark   Medium   Light   Black

STRIPPLE STAR

COLOR PHOTO
ON PAGE 54.

FINISHED QUILT SIZE
51" x 62¼"

FINISHED BLOCK SIZE
8" x 8"

Block A

Block B

Block C

Block D

Block E

 Red print

Dark blue print

Medium blue print

Light blue print

Gray print

MATERIALS: 44"-WIDE FABRIC

1 yd. red print
1 yd. dark blue print
1 yd. medium blue print
1⅞ yds. light blue print
1⅝ yds. gray print
½ yd. binding
4 yds. backing

61

CUTTING

All measurements include ¼"-wide seam allowances.

From the red print, cut:

1 piece, 9½" x 42", for Strip Unit II

2 pieces, each 9½" x 42"; crosscut into:

    1 piece, 9½" x 31", for Strip Unit II

    2 squares, each 9½" x 9½", for Strip Unit III

From *each* of the dark and medium blue prints, cut:

2 pieces, each 9½" x 42", for Strip Units II and IV

1 piece, 9½" x 42"; crosscut into:

    1 piece, 9½" x 22", for Strip Unit II

    5 squares, each 4⅛" x 4⅛", for Blocks D and E piecing

From the light blue print, cut:

5 strips, each 2½" x 42", for Strip Unit I

4 pieces, each 9½" x 42", for Strip Units II and IV

1 piece, 9½" x 42"; crosscut into:

    2 squares, each 9½" x 9½", for Strip Unit IV

    10 squares, each 4⅛" x 4⅛", for Blocks D and E piecing

From the gray print, cut:

5 strips, each 2½" x 42", for Strip Unit I

1 piece, 9½" x 42"; crosscut into:

    4 squares, each 9½" x 9½", for Strip Unit III

5 strips, each 4½" x 42"; crosscut into:

    4 rectangles, each 4½" x 8½", for Block C piecing

    4 rectangles, each 2½" x 4½", for Block C piecing

    34 squares, each 4½" x 4½", for Blocks B and D piecing

3 strips, each 2½" x 42"; crosscut into:

    48 squares, each 2½" x 2½", for Blocks B and C piecing

From the fabric for binding, cut;

6 strips, each 2" x 42"

Refer to the instructions on page 19 for cutting Method Two bias strips.

Using the Bias Stripper, cut the size and number of full bias strips indicated in the chart. Cut all fabrics face down. If you are left-handed, cut all fabrics face up. Reserve the leftover 9½" corner triangles for use later in the quilt.

FABRIC	NO. OF PIECES	SIZE	CUTTING MARK	TOTAL NO. FULL BIAS STRIPS	STRIP UNIT
Red	1	9½" x 42"	2¾"	9	II
	1	9½" x 31"	2¾"	6	II
Dk. Blue	1	9½" x 42"	2¾"	9	IV
	1	9½" x 42"	1"	18	II
	1	9½" x 22"	1"	7	II
Med. Blue	1	9½" x 42"	2¾"	9	IV
	1	9½" x 42"	1"	18	II
	1	9½" x 22"	1"	7	II
Lt. Blue	4	9½" x 42"	2¾"	33	II, IV

Red   Dark blue   Medium blue   Light blue   Gray

Piecing the Blocks

Refer to the instructions on pages 19–21 for making striped rectangles, and pages 17–22 for making Method One and Method Two bias squares. Press seam allowances in the direction of the arrows unless otherwise instructed.

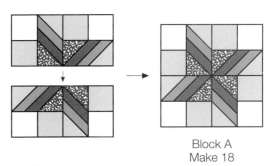

Block A
Make 18

Block A

1. Using 5 light blue and 5 gray 2½" x 42" strips, assemble 5 Strip Unit I. Cut a total of 72 segments, each 2½" wide, from Strip Unit I.

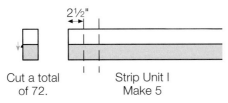

2½"

Cut a total
of 72.

Strip Unit I
Make 5

2. Assemble 5 Strip Unit II. Cut a total of 72 striped rectangles, each 2½" x 4½", from Strip Unit II.

Strip Unit II
Make 5

Cut a total of 72.

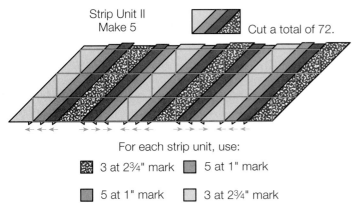

For each strip unit, use:

3 at 2¾" mark   5 at 1" mark

5 at 1" mark   3 at 2¾" mark

3. Sew a segment from Strip Unit I to each striped rectangle.

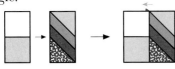

Make 72

4. Turning one unit on its side, sew 2 units from step 3 together to make a half block.

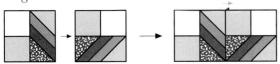

Make 36

5. Sew 2 half blocks together to complete Block A. Press the final seam in either direction.

Block B

1. Cut the 4 gray and 2 red 9½" squares once diagonally to yield 8 gray triangles and 4 red triangles. Add the 4 reserved red 9½" corner triangles to the stack. Pair each gray triangle with a red triangle, placing right sides together and aligning the long edges. Cut the triangle pairs into Method One bias strips at the 2¾" mark. See page 22. You will get 1 pair of tall strips and 1 pair of short strips from each pair of triangles.

2. Sew the pairs of bias strips on the long edges and join the same length pairs to make 1 tall and 1 short Strip Unit III. Cut a total of 56 bias squares, each 2½" x 2½", from Strip Unit III.

Strip Unit III
Make 1 tall strip unit
and 1 short strip unit.

Cut a total of 56.

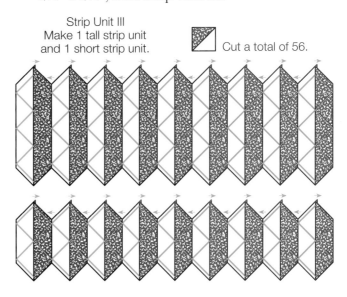

3. Sew a red/gray bias square to a 2½" gray square to make Type A and Type B units.

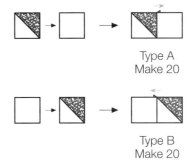

Type A
Make 20

Type B
Make 20

 Red   Dark blue   Medium blue   Light blue   Gray

4. Sew a Type A unit to a Type B unit to make a four-patch unit.

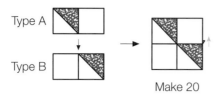

Make 20

5. Sew a four-patch unit to the left side of a 4½" gray square to make a C unit. Sew a four-patch unit to the right side of a 4½" gray square to make a D unit.

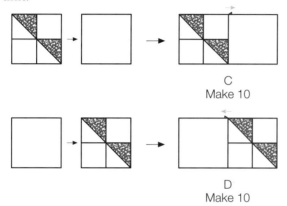

C
Make 10

D
Make 10

6. Sew a C and a D unit together to complete Block B.

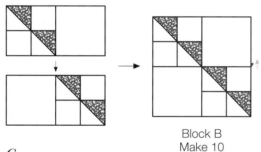

Block B
Make 10

Block C

1. Sew a red/gray bias square to each end of a 2½" x 4½" gray rectangle.

Make 4

2. Re-press 4 of the remaining red/gray bias squares so that the seams are pressed toward the gray instead of toward the red. Sew these to the right side of a bias square pressed toward the red.

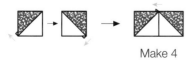

Make 4

3. Sew a 2½" gray square to opposite ends of a unit made in step 2.

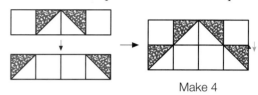

Make 4

4. Sew a unit from step 1 to a unit from step 3.

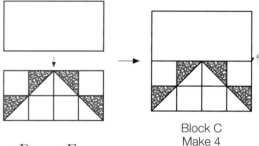

Make 4

5. Sew a 4½" x 8½" gray rectangle to the top of a unit from step 4 to complete Block C.

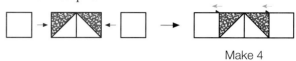

Block C
Make 4

Blocks D and E

1. Cut the 2 light blue 9½" squares once diagonally to yield 4 triangles.
2. Cut 2 reserved dark blue corner triangles, 1 reserved medium blue corner triangle, and 3 of the 4 light blue triangles cut in step 1 into Method One bias strips at the 2¾" mark. See page 22. Set aside the fourth light blue triangle for step 4 at right.
3. Using 9 dark blue, 9 medium blue, and 18 light blue full bias strips cut at the 2¾" mark, plus the Method One bias strips cut in step 2, assemble 3 Strip Unit IV. See "Reusing Method Two Corner Triangles" on page 22. Please note that the dark and medium blue strips are used interchangeably as if they were one print. They are alternated randomly in the strip unit with the light blue for a dark/light effect. Cut a total of 115 bias squares, each 2½" x 2½", from Strip Unit IV.

Strip Unit IV
Make 3

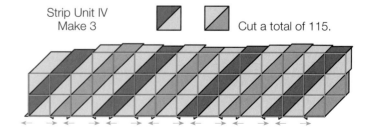

Cut a total of 115.

Red   Dark blue   Medium blue   Light blue   Gray

4. Using the remaining 9 leftover light blue 9½" triangles, 5 dark blue 9½" triangles, and 4 medium blue 9½" triangles, pair each light blue triangle with a dark blue or medium blue triangle, placing right sides together and aligning the long edges. Cut the triangle pairs into bias strips at the 2¾" mark. Sew the pairs on the long edges and join the same-length pairs to make 1 tall and 1 short Strip Unit V. Cut a total of 69 bias squares, each 2½" x 2½", from Strip Unit V. You should now have a total of 184 blue bias squares.

Strip Unit V
Make 1 tall strip unit
and 1 short strip unit.

Cut a total of 69.

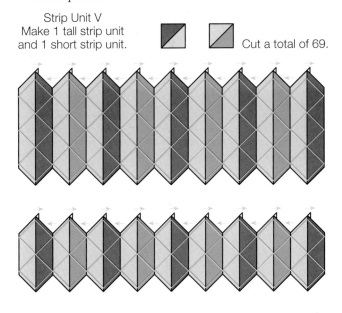

5. Sew 144 of the blue bias squares into 72 pairs. Sew the pairs together to make 36 pinwheel units. Use the dark blue/light blue and medium blue/light blue bias squares randomly for a dark/light effect.

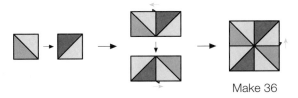

Make 36

6. Cut 5 dark blue, 5 medium blue, and 10 light blue 4⅛" squares twice diagonally to yield 80 quarter-square triangles (40 light blue, 20 dark blue, and 20 medium blue).

7. Sew a dark or medium blue triangle from step 6 to the top of each of the remaining 40 blue 2½" bias squares. The dark blue and medium blue triangles are used interchangeably as if they were one print. Sew a light blue triangle to the right side of the unit to make a pieced triangle.

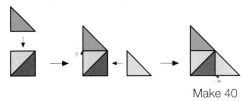

Make 40

TIP

When sewing a triangle to a square, always start sewing the seam from the side with the square corner of the triangle.

Stitch from
this corner.

8. Using the pieced triangles, pinwheel units, and 4½" gray squares, assemble Block D.

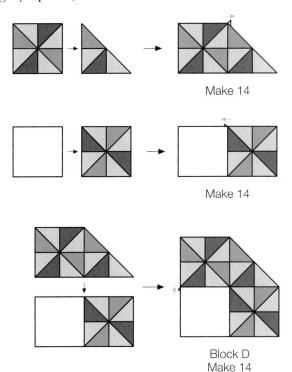

Make 14

Make 14

Block D
Make 14

Red   Dark blue   Medium blue   Light blue   Gray

9. Sew the remaining 8 pinwheel units into 4 pairs.

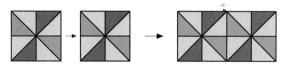

Make 4

10. Sew a pieced triangle to opposite sides of a pinwheel pair.

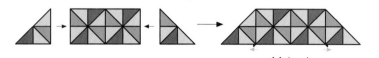

Make 4

11. Sew 8 of the remaining pieced triangles together into 4 pairs.

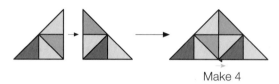

Make 4

12. Sew a pieced triangle pair to the top of each unit made in step 10 to complete Block E. Press final seam in either direction. These are the pieced corners for the quilt.

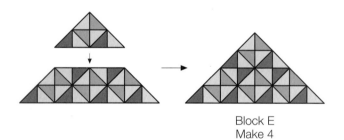

Block E
Make 4

Assembling and Finishing the Quilt Top

1. Lay out the 18 Block A, 10 Block B, 4 Block C, 14 Block D, and the remaining 10 pieced triangles as shown. Sew the blocks and pieced triangles together in diagonal rows. Press seams in opposite directions from row to row.

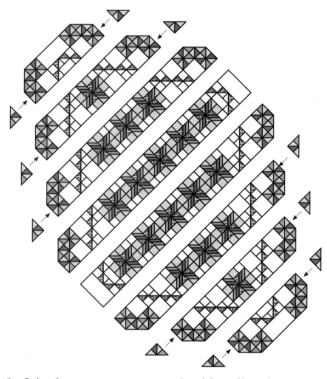

2. Join the rows; press seams in either direction.
3. Sew a Block E to each of the 4 corners to complete the quilt top.
4. Refer to the general directions for quilt finishing, beginning on page 95. Layer the completed quilt top with batting and backing; baste. Quilt as desired. Bind the edges of the quilt. Label the quilt.

 Red   Dark blue   Medium blue   Light blue   Gray

MOUNTAIN FIRE

COLOR PHOTO
ON PAGE 56.

FINISHED QUILT SIZE
72½" x 72½"

FINISHED BLOCK SIZE
10" x 10"

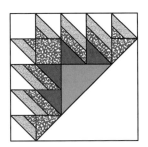

Mountain Fire

- ■ Black print
- ▨ Red prints
- ▧ Gold/orange prints
- ▨ Dark gray print
- □ Medium gray print

MATERIALS: 44"-WIDE FABRIC

2⅛ yds. black print
½ yd. each of 4 red prints   *red*
⅝ yd. each of 3 gold-orange prints   *purple*
1⅜ yds. dark gray print   *print*
1¾ yds. medium gray print   *yellow*
⅝ yd. binding
4½ yds. backing

67

CUTTING

All measurements include ¼"-wide seam allowances.

From the black print, cut:
2 pieces, each 9" x 42", for Strip Units I and II
2 pieces, each 9" x 42"; crosscut into:
    8 squares, each 9" x 9", for Strip Unit V
    4 squares, each 2½" x 2½", for pieced border
        corner squares
8 strips, each 4½" x 42", for outer border

From *each* of the red prints, cut:
1 piece, 9" x 42"; crosscut into:
2 pieces, each 9" x 21", for Strip Units I, II, III,
    and IV
1 strip, 2⅞" x 42"; crosscut into:
    6 squares, each 2⅞" x 2⅞", for block piecing
    6 squares, each 2½" x 2½", for block piecing

From *each* of the gold-orange prints, cut:
2 pieces, each 9" x 29", for Strip Units I, II, III, and
    IV

From the dark gray print, cut:
2 strips, each 15½" x 42"; crosscut into:
    4 squares, each 15½" x 15½", for side
        triangles and corners
    12 squares, each 4⅞" x 4⅞", for block
        piecing
6 strips, each 2¼" x 42", for inner border

From the medium gray print, cut:
4 pieces, each 9" x 42", for Strip Units I, II, III, and
    IV
2 strips, each 2½" x 42"; crosscut into:
    24 squares, each 2½" x 2½", for block
        piecing
2 strips, each 8⅞" x 42"; crosscut into:
    8 squares, each 8⅞" x 8⅞", for block piecing

From the fabric for binding, cut:
8 strips, each 2" x 42"

Bias Strip Cutting Chart

Refer to the instructions on page 19 for cutting Method Two bias strips.

Using the Bias Stripper, cut the size and number of bias strips indicated in the chart. Pay attention to fabric direction when cutting. Reserve all the 9" leftover corner triangles for use later in the quilt.

FABRIC	NO. OF PIECES	SIZE	FABRIC DIRECTION	CUTTING MARK	NO. OF STRIPS FROM EACH PIECE	TOTAL NO. FULL BIAS STRIPS	STRIP UNIT
Black	1	9" x 42"	face up	2¾"	9	9	I
	1	9" x 42"	face down	2¾"	9	9	II
Reds	4	9" x 21"	face up	1"	4	16	I
				1¾"	2	8	III
	4	9" x 21"	face down	1"	4	16	II
				1¾"	2	8	IV
Gold/Orange	3	9" x 29"	face up	1"	11	32	I, III
	3	9" x 29"	face down	1"	11	32	II, IV
Med. Gray	2	9" x 42"	face up	2¾"	9	18	I, III
	2	9" x 42"	face down	2¾"	9	18	II, IV

 Black   Red   Gold/orange   Dark gray   ☐ Medium gray

Piecing the Blocks

Refer to pages 19–21 for making pieced rectangles and striped squares. Press all seams in the direction of the arrows unless otherwise instructed.

1. Assemble 2 variations of Strip Unit I. Cut a total of 48 striped rectangles, each $2\frac{1}{2}$" x $4\frac{1}{2}$", from Strip Unit I.

Strip Unit I
Make 1 of each type.

Cut a total of 48.

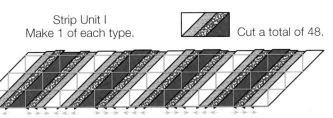

Use face-down strips:

■ 4 at $2\frac{3}{4}$" mark   ■ 8 at 1" mark

▨ 8 at 1" mark   □ 5 at $2\frac{3}{4}$" mark

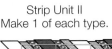

Use face-down strips:

■ 5 at $2\frac{3}{4}$" mark   ■ 8 at 1" mark

▨ 8 at 1" mark   □ 4 at $2\frac{3}{4}$" mark

2. Assemble 2 variations of Strip Unit II. Cut a total of 48 striped rectangles, each $2\frac{1}{2}$" x $4\frac{1}{2}$", from Strip Unit II.

Strip Unit II
Make 1 of each type.

Cut a total of 48.

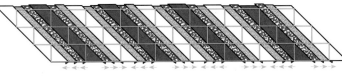

Use face-up strips:

■ 4 at $2\frac{3}{4}$" mark   ▨ 8 at 1" mark

▨ 8 at 1" mark   □ 5 at $2\frac{3}{4}$" mark

Use face-up strips:

■ 5 at $2\frac{3}{4}$" mark   ▨ 8 at 1" mark

▨ 8 at 1" mark   □ 4 at $2\frac{3}{4}$" mark

3. Assemble 1 Strip Unit III. Cut 48 striped squares, each $2\frac{1}{2}$" x $2\frac{1}{2}$", from Strip Unit III.

Strip Unit III
Make 1

Cut 48

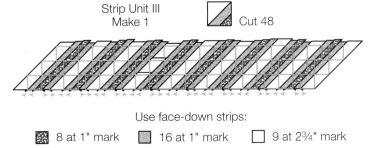

Use face-down strips:

▨ 8 at 1" mark   ▨ 16 at 1" mark   □ 9 at $2\frac{3}{4}$" mark

4. Assemble 1 Strip Unit IV. Cut 48 striped squares, each $2\frac{1}{2}$" x $2\frac{1}{2}$", from Strip Unit IV.

Strip Unit IV
Make 1

Cut 48

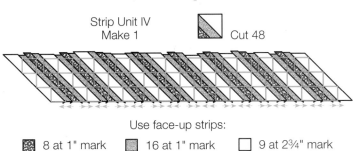

Use face-up strips:

▨ 8 at 1" mark   ▨ 16 at 1" mark   □ 9 at $2\frac{3}{4}$" mark

5. Join a $2\frac{1}{2}$" medium gray square, a $2\frac{1}{2}$" red square, and 2 striped squares to make a corner unit.

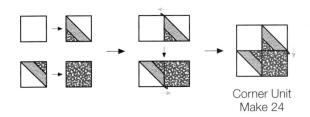

Corner Unit
Make 24

6. Sew the 48 Strip Unit I striped rectangles into pairs.

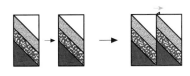

Make 24

7. Sew a striped rectangle pair to the right side of a corner unit.

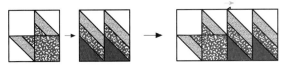

Make 24

 Black   Red   Gold/orange   Dark gray   □ Medium gray

8. Cut the 24 red 2⅞" squares once diagonally to yield 48 half-square triangles. Nub each triangle to 2½". See "Nubbing Half-Square Triangles" on page 10. Sew a red triangle to the side of a striped square as shown to make a right end unit.

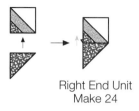

Right End Unit
Make 24

9. Sew a right end unit to the right side of a striped rectangle unit from step 7.

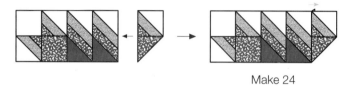

Make 24

10. Sew the 48 Strip Unit II striped rectangles into pairs.

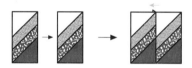

Make 24

11. Sew a red triangle to the side of a striped square as shown to make a left end unit. They are different from those made in step 8.

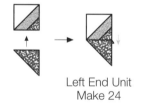

Left End Unit
Make 24

12. Sew a left end unit to the left side of a Strip Unit II striped rectangle pair.

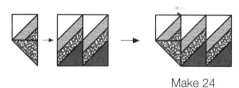

Make 24

13. Cut the 12 dark gray 4⅞" squares once diagonally to yield 24 half-square triangles. Nub each triangle to 4½". See "Nubbing Half-Square Triangles" on page 10. Sew a dark gray triangle to the side of the striped rectangle unit made in step 12.

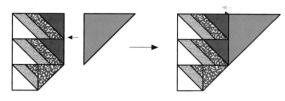

Make 24

14. Sew the Strip Unit I striped rectangle unit from step 9 to the top of the rectangle/dark gray triangle unit to complete a half block.

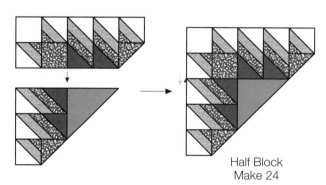

Half Block
Make 24

15. Cut the 8 medium gray 8⅞" squares once diagonally to yield 16 half-square triangles. Nub each triangle to 8½". Nub and resize the 8 medium gray 9" leftover corner triangles to 8½". See "Nubbing Half-Square Triangles" on page 10. Sew a medium gray triangle to a half block to complete a Mountain Fire block. Press the final seam toward the medium gray triangles.

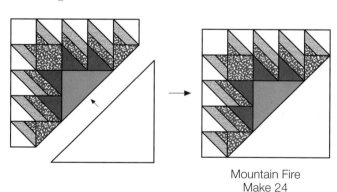

Mountain Fire
Make 24

■ Black   ▨ Red   ▨ Gold/orange   ▨ Dark gray   □ Medium gray

Assembling and Finishing the Quilt Top

1. Cut 2 dark gray 15½" squares twice diagonally to yield 8 side triangles. Cut the remaining dark gray squares once diagonally to yield 4 corner triangles.

2. Arrange the 24 Mountain Fire blocks and the 8 dark gray side triangles in rows as shown below. Sew the blocks and triangles together in diagonal rows. Press seams in opposite directions from row to row.

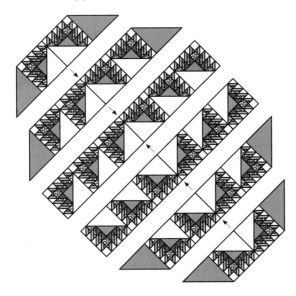

3. Join the rows; press seams in either direction. Add a corner triangle to each corner.

4. Trim the quilt top to ¼" from the block corners. See page 95.

5. Attach the 2¼"-wide dark gray inner border to the quilt top, following the directions for "Plain Borders" on page 95.

6. Choose 20 of your favorite reserved red and gold-orange 9" corner triangles. Select the triangles that are closest to 9" in size on the 2 short sides (½" more or less won't matter). Cut the 8 black 9" squares once diagonally to yield 16 triangles. Add the 4 reserved black 9" corner triangles for a total of 20 black triangles.

7. Pair each red and gold-orange 9" triangle with a black 9" triangle, placing right sides together and aligning the long edges. Cut the triangle pairs into bias strips at the 2¾" mark. See page 22. You will have 1 tall and 1 short pair of strips from each triangle pair.

8. Sew pairs of bias strips on the long edges and join the same-length pairs together to make 1 tall and 1 short Strip Unit V. If the strips are slightly different in length, line up one end when stitching and leave the other end ragged. Cut a total of 120 bias squares,

each 2½" x 2½", from Strip Unit V. Cut from the even side of each strip unit. You may have more bias squares than you need. Set aside the extras for a pieced backing or another project.

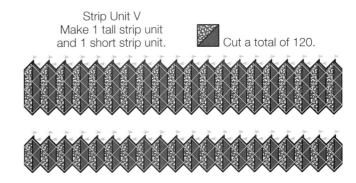

Strip Unit V
Make 1 tall strip unit
and 1 short strip unit.   Cut a total of 120.

9. Sew 15 bias squares together to make 4 left half-rows, and 15 bias squares together to make 4 right half-rows. Join a left half-row to a right half-row so that the black triangles meet in the center. Press center seams open. Make 4 pieced middle borders.

Make 4 Left Half Rows.

Make 4 Right Half Rows.

10. Measure the width and length of the quilt top and the pieced middle border strips. If they all measure 60½", no adjustments are necessary. If not, take in or let out the pieced borders a little bit on a few seams to bring it to the same size as the quilt top. See "Pieced Borders" on page 95.

11. Sew 2 of the pieced borders to opposite sides of the quilt top and press the seams toward the black border. The red triangles should point away from the center of the quilt. Refer to quilt plan on page 67.

12. Sew a 2½" black square to each end of the remaining pieced borders. Press the seams toward the squares. Sew the border strips to the top and bottom edges of the quilt top and press the seams toward the black border. Remember to orient the red triangles in the same direction as the side borders.

13. Attach the 4½"-wide black outer border to the quilt top, following the directions for "Plain Borders" on page 95.

14. Refer to the general directions for quilt finishing, beginning on page 95. Layer the completed quilt top with batting and backing; baste. Quilt as desired. Bind the edges of the quilt. Label the quilt.

 Black   Red   Gold/orange Dark gray Medium gray

COLOR PHOTO
ON PAGE 77.

FINISHED QUILT SIZE
38½" x 42½"

FINISHED HOUSE
BLOCK SIZE 6" x 6"

FINISHED TREE
BLOCK SIZE 4" x 6"

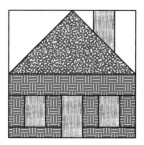

House Block

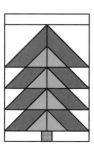

Tree Block

This is truly a humble little quilt since it is easily made from fabric scraps you may have on hand. Even though fabric requirements are given for the greens and tans, you can ignore them and use the cutting instructions as a guide to cut each 7½"-wide piece from a different print that you may already have.

- Dark green prints
- Medium green prints
- Tan prints
- Brown print
- Asst. prints for houses
- Asst. prints for roofs
- Asst. prints for chimneys, doors, and windows

MATERIALS: 44"-WIDE FABRIC

¼ yd. or 1 fat quarter each of 5 dark green prints
¼ yd. or 1 fat quarter each of 4 medium green prints
¼ yd. or 1 fat quarter each of 5 tan prints
2" x 15" or 3" x 8" piece of brown print
8" x 8" piece for each house
4" x 7" piece for each roof
assorted 3" square scraps for the chimneys, doors, and windows
½ yd. of tan print for inner border
⅝ yd. of green plaid for outer border
⅜ yd. binding
1½ yds. backing

CUTTING

All measurements include ¼"-wide seam allowances.

From *each* of the 5 dark green and 4 medium green prints, cut:
2 pieces, each 7½" x 12¾", for Strip Units I, II, III, and IV

From *each* of the 5 tan prints, cut:
2 pieces, each 7½" x 13½", for Strip Units I, II, III, and IV
2 pieces, each 1" x 4½", for Tree block piecing

From any of the assorted tan leftovers, cut these additional pieces:
2 strips, each 1" x 4½", for Tree block piecing
3 squares, each 3⅞" x 3⅞", for House block piecing
4 strips, each 2¼" x 7", for Strip Unit V
4 strips, each 1½" x 6½", for quilt-row ends

From the brown print, cut:
2 strips, each 1" x 7", for Strip Unit V

From *each* house print, cut:
1 bar, 1½" x 6½", for house (over the windows)
2 bars, each 1" x 3", for house (under the windows)
4 bars, each 1¼" x 2", for house (between the windows)

From *each* roof print, cut:
1 rectangle, 3½" x 6½", for roof

From the assorted chimney, window, and door scraps for each house, cut:
1 bar, 1½" x 3", for chimney
2 bars, each 1½" x 2", for windows
1 bar, 1½" x 2½", for door

From the tan print for the inner border, cut:
4 strips, each 2½" x 42"

From the green plaid for the outer border, cut:
4 strips, each 4½" x 42"

From the fabric for binding, cut:
5 strips, each 2" x 42"

Bias Strip Cutting Chart

Refer to the instructions on page 19 for cutting Method Two bias strips.

Using the Bias Stripper, cut the number and size of full bias strips indicated in the chart. Pay attention to fabric direction when cutting. Reserve all twenty of the tan leftover corner triangles for use later in the quilt. Set aside the dark and medium green leftover corner triangles for a pieced backing or another project.

FABRIC	NO. OF PIECES	SIZE	FABRIC DIRECTION	CUTTING MARK	NO. OF STRIPS FROM EACH PIECE	TOTAL NO. FULL BIAS STRIPS	STRIP UNIT
Dk. greens	5	7½" x 12¾"	face up	1"	3	15	I, III
	5	7½" x 12¾"	face down	1"	3	15	II, IV
Med. greens	4	7½" x 12¾"	face up	1¾"	2	8	I, III
	4	7½" x 12¾"	face down	1¾"	2	8	II, IV
Tans	5	7½" x 13½"	face up	1¾"	1	5	I
				2¾"	1	4	III
	5	7½" x 13½"	face down	1¾"	1	5	II
				2¾"	1	4	IV

■ Dark green ■ Medium green □ Tan ▨ Brown ▦ Asst. prints for houses ▨ Asst. prints for roofs ▨ Asst. prints for chimneys, doors, and windows

PIECING THE BLOCKS

Refer to the instructions on pages 19–21 for making striped rectangles and striped squares. Press seam allowances in the direction of the arrows unless otherwise instructed.

TREE BLOCKS

1. Assemble Strip Unit I. Cut 36 striped rectangles, each $1\frac{1}{2}$" x $2\frac{1}{2}$", from Strip Unit I.

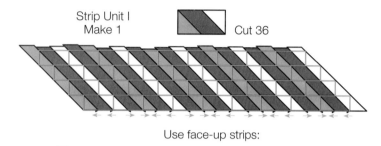

Strip Unit I
Make 1   Cut 36

Use face-up strips:

■ 9 at 1" mark   ■ 5 at 1¾" mark   □ 5 at 1¾" mark

2. Assemble Strip Unit II. Cut 36 striped rectangles, each $1\frac{1}{2}$" x $2\frac{1}{2}$", from Strip Unit II.

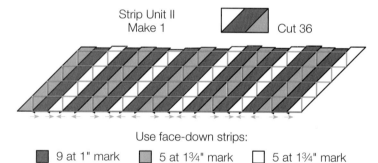

Strip Unit II
Make 1   Cut 36

Use face-down strips:

■ 9 at 1" mark   ■ 5 at 1¾" mark   □ 5 at 1¾" mark

3. Assemble Strip Unit III. Cut 12 striped squares, each $2\frac{1}{2}$" x $2\frac{1}{2}$", from Strip Unit III.

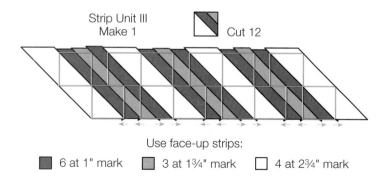

Strip Unit III
Make 1   Cut 12

Use face-up strips:

■ 6 at 1" mark   ■ 3 at 1¾" mark   □ 4 at 2¾" mark

4. Assemble Strip Unit IV. Cut 12 striped squares, each $2\frac{1}{2}$" x $2\frac{1}{2}$", from Strip Unit IV.

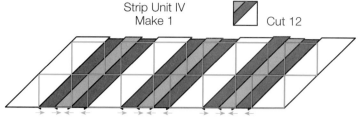

Strip Unit IV
Make 1   Cut 12

Use face-down strips:

■ 6 at 1" mark   ■ 3 at 1¾" mark   □ 4 at 2¾" mark

5. Sew a $2\frac{1}{4}$" x 7" straight-grain tan strip to opposite sides of a 1" x 7" brown strip. Make 2 Strip Unit V. Cut a total of 12 segments, each 1" wide, from Strip Unit V for the tree trunks.

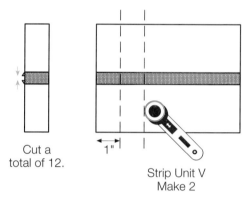

Cut a
total of 12.   1"

Strip Unit V
Make 2

6. Assemble the tree, following the piecing diagram.

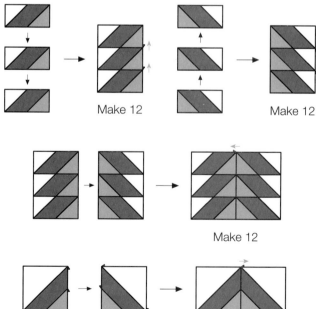

Make 12   Make 12

Make 12

Strip Unit IV   Strip Unit III   Make 12

■ Dark green   ■ Medium green   □ Tan   ▨ Brown   ▦ Asst. prints for houses   ▨ Asst. prints for roofs   ▧ Asst. prints for chimneys, doors, and windows

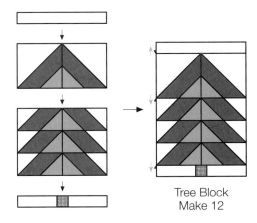

Tree Block
Make 12

HOUSE BLOCKS

1. Cut the 3 tan 3⅞" squares once diagonally to yield 6 triangles for the roof unit. Cut another 20 triangles, each 3⅞", from the 20 reserved 7" tan corner triangles, using Judy Hopkins's ScrapMaster. See pages 9–10 for directions on using the ScrapMaster. (If you do not have a ScrapMaster, you can nub and resize the corner triangles to 3½", following the instructions for "Nubbing Half-Square Triangles" on page 10.)

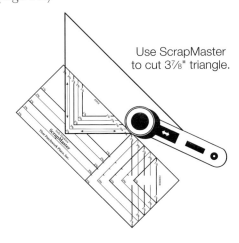

Use ScrapMaster
to cut 3⅞" triangle.

Note: The following instructions are to make 1 House block. Repeat the process to make all 13 houses.

2. Cut a 1½" strip from a 3⅞" tan triangle. Save the cutaway triangle.

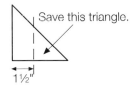

Save this triangle.

1½"

3. Sew a 1½" x 3" chimney bar to the short side of the strip cut in step 2. Sew the cutaway triangle back in place on the other side of the chimney bar.

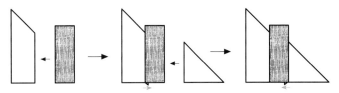

4. Use the ScrapMaster to recut the pieced chimney triangle to 3⅞". Nub the pieced triangle to 3½". See "Nubbing Half-Square Triangles" on page 10.

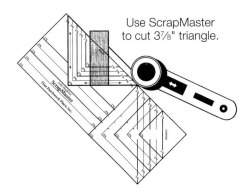

Use ScrapMaster
to cut 3⅞" triangle.

5. With right sides together, pin a plain, nubbed 3½" tan triangle to the left side of the 3½" x 6½" roof rectangle. Since the triangle is nubbed, the corners should align with the sides of the rectangle. Stitch ¼" from the long edge of the triangle. Trim background fabric ¼" from the stitching line.

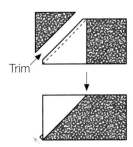

Trim

6. Follow the same procedure in step 5 to sew the pieced chimney triangle to the right side of the roof.

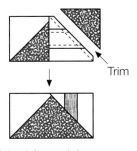

Trim

Make 1 for each house.

 Dark green   Medium green   Tan   Brown   Asst. prints for houses Asst. prints for roofs Asst. prints for chimneys, doors, and windows

7. Assemble a House block, following the piecing diagram.

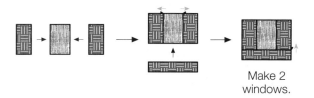

Make 2 windows.

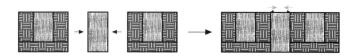

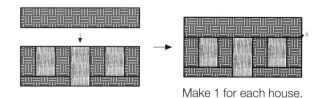

Make 1 for each house.

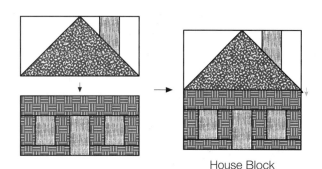

House Block

8. Repeat steps 2–7 to make 12 more House blocks.

ASSEMBLING AND FINISHING THE QUILT TOP

1. Assemble 3 rows, using 3 House blocks and 2 Tree blocks for each row.

Make 3 rows.

2. Assemble 2 rows, using 3 Tree blocks, 2 House blocks, and 2 tan $1\frac{1}{2}$" x $6\frac{1}{2}$" bars for each row.

1½" x 6½" tan bar
1½" x 6½" tan bar

Make 2 rows.

3. Join the rows as shown in the quilt plan on page 72. The seams should butt between the bottom of the House blocks and the top of the chimneys. Press seams joining the rows in either direction.

4. Attach the $2\frac{1}{2}$"-wide inner border to the quilt, following the directions for "Plain Borders" on page 95. Repeat for the $4\frac{1}{2}$"-wide outer border.

5. Refer to the general directions for quilt finishing, beginning on page 95. Layer the completed quilt top with batting and backing; baste. Quilt as desired. Bind the edges of the quilt. Label the quilt.

 Dark green   Medium green   Tan   Brown   Asst. prints for houses   Asst. prints for roofs   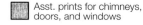 Asst. prints for chimneys, doors, and windows

Be It Ever So Humble...
by Donna Lynn Thomas,
1994, Lansing, Kansas,
38½" x 42½".
Warm, cozy, and plaid, this charming quilt is made easily from scraps and fabrics on hand. Bias strip piecing makes the trees a breeze to put together. Machine quilted by Kari Lane. Directions begin on page 72.

Fences

by Donna Lynn Thomas, 1994, Lansing, Kansas, 78½" x 94½".

Twelve blocks interlock to form a fascinating design. The fancy ribbon pieced border frames the center and floats it on a cream-colored "canvas." Beautifully hand quilted by Aline Duerr and Norma Jean Rohman. Directions begin on page 81.

The Facts of Life

by Gabriel Pursell, 1994, Leavenworth, Kansas, 68" x 84".

Gabriel made this happy, delightful quilt for her twelve-year-old daughter, Hannah. The bright, cheerful colors in flower and egg prints are perfect for the room of a young girl entering her teen years. Gabriel eliminated the pieced border to keep the quilt to the dimensions of her daughter's bed. Machine quilted by Kari Lane.

Royal Beauty

by Donna Lynn Thomas, 1994, Lansing, Kansas, 91¼" x 91¼"

A variation of Blackford's Beauty, Royal Beauty undulates with gradations of royal purples and olive greens. Setting the blocks together on point highlights the effect. The side setting triangles are exquisitely quilted with a padded feather design, and the borders are quilted by following the motif in the print. Machine quilted by Betty Gilliam. Directions begin on page 88.

Twilight Garden

by M. Deborah Rose, 1994, Ft. Leavenworth, Kansas, 91¼" x 91¼".

From the rich colors to the beautiful hand quilting, this quilt evokes elegance. It should be no surprise that Deborah is the daughter of Aline Duerr and the niece of Norma Jean Rohman.

Crossing Paths
**by Beth Wagenaar,
1995, Ft. Leavenworth,
Kansas,
63" x 87".**

*The simple Sawtooth Square
block creates an exciting overall
design when set together this
way. Study the quilt for a
moment and you'll start to
notice all kinds of secondary
designs—spools, variable stars,
baskets, and a wonderful
diagonal effect. Beth named
this quilt in honor of her ten-
month stay at Ft. Leavenworth,
where she has happily crossed
paths with many, many friends
from previous tours of duty.
Directions begin on page 92.*

*Rather than buy fabric for
a backing, Beth pieced a large
Rail Fence quilt for her
backing, using extra fabric she
had on hand.*

FENCES

COLOR PHOTO ON
PAGE 78.

FINISHED QUILT SIZE
78½" x 94½"

FINISHED BLOCK SIZE
16" x 16"

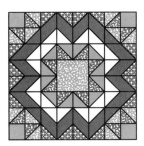

Fences

■ Dark green print

■ Medium green print

▨ Light floral print

□ Tan print

▨ Dark red print

▨ Medium red print

This intricate-looking design is much simpler to construct than it may seem, since it is almost completely strip pieced. Consider that, if you made this quilt in the traditional manner using individually cut pieces, each block would be composed of 101 individual pieces! By using bias strip piecing, you cut and sew only 45 units to make each block. Not only that, as a result of bias strip-piecing techniques, the accuracy of each unit is nearly perfect. It still takes time to put this quilt top together, but the block piecing is frustration-free, making it a pleasure to assemble.

MATERIALS: 44"-WIDE FABRIC

2⅛ yds. dark green print
1½ yds. medium green print
2⅝ yds. light floral print
3 yds. tan print
1⅛ yds. dark red print
1⅛ yds. medium red print
1⅝ yds. dark green border print
⅝ yd. binding
5¾ yds. backing

CUTTING

All measurements include ¼"-wide seam allowances.

From the dark green print, cut:
6 pieces, each 12" x 42", for Strip Units I and II
From the medium green print, cut:
1 piece, 12" x 42", for Strip Unit IV
1 piece, 12" x 29", for Strip Unit VIII
1 piece, 12" x 38", for Strip Units IV and VII
1 piece, 12" x 42"; crosscut into:
    1 square, 12" x 12", for Strip Unit V
    48 squares, each 2½" x 2½", for block piecing
From the tan print, cut:
4 pieces, each 12" x 42", for Strip Units I and II
2 pieces, each 12" x 42"; crosscut into:
    2 pieces, each 12" x 26", for Strip Units VII
      and VIII
    4 squares, each 4½" x 4½", for pieced border
      (second border)
8 strips, each 3½" x 42", for third border

From the light floral print, cut:
6 pieces, each 12" x 42", for Strip Units I, II, VII,
    and VIII
6 strips, each 2½" x 42", for first border
From the dark red print, cut:
2 pieces, each 12" x 42", for Strip Units III and IV
1 piece, 12" x 26", for Strip Units III and IV
From the medium red print, cut:
1 piece, 12" x 42", for Strip Unit III
2 pieces, each 12" x 42"; crosscut into:
    1 piece, 12" x 19", for Strip Unit III
    2 squares, each 12" x 12", for Strip Unit VI
    12 squares, each 4½" x 4½", for block piecing
From the dark green border print, cut:
8 strips, each 6½" x 42", for fourth border
From the fabric for binding, cut:
9 strips, each 2" x 42"

 Dark green   Medium green   Light floral   Tan   Dark red   Medium red

Bias Strip

Cutting

Chart

Refer to the instructions on page 19 for cutting Method Two bias strips.

Using the Bias Stripper, cut the number and size of full bias strips indicated in the chart from the assorted 12"-wide fabric pieces. Pay attention to fabric direction when cutting. If you are left-handed, cut all fabrics in the opposite direction from that stated in the chart.

FABRIC	NO. OF PIECES	SIZE	FABRIC DIRECTION	CUTTING MARK	TOTAL NO. FULL BIAS STRIPS	STRIP UNIT
Dark green	3	12" x 42"	face up	2"	32	I
	3	12" x 42"	face down	2"	32	II
Light floral	3	12" x 42"	face up	2¾"	24	I, VII
	3	12" x 42"	face down	2¾"	24	II, VIII
Tan	2	12" x 42"	face up	2¾"	16	I
	1	12" x 26"	face up	2¾"	4	VII
	2	12" x 42"	face down	2¾"	16	II
	1	12" x 26"	face down	2¾"	4	VIII
Med. green	1	12" x 38"	face up	2"	7	VII
				2¾"	2	IV
	1	12" x 29"	face down	2"	7	VIII
	1	12" x 42"	face up	2¾"	8	IV
Dk. red	2	12" x 42"	face up	2¾"	16	III, IV
	1	12" x 26"	face up	2¾"	4	III, IV
Med. red	1	12" x 42"	face up	2¾"	8	III
	1	12" x 19"	face up	2¾"	2	III

Reserve the following leftover 12" corner triangles for use later. Set aside remaining leftover corner triangles for a pieced backing or another project.

    5 dark green triangles for Strip Unit VI
    5 tan triangles for Strip Unit V
    5 medium green triangles for Strip Unit IV and V
    4 dark red triangles for Strip Units III and IV
    3 medium red triangles for Strip Unit III and VI

 Dark green   Medium green   Light floral   Tan   Dark red   Medium red

PIECING THE BLOCKS

Refer to the instructions on pages 19–21 for making striped rectangles, and pages 17–22 for making bias squares. Press seam allowances in the direction of the arrows unless otherwise instructed.

1. Assemble 4 Strip Unit I. Cut a total of 128 striped rectangles, each 2¹⁄₂" x 4¹⁄₂", from Strip Unit I. Set aside 32 striped rectangles for the pieced border.

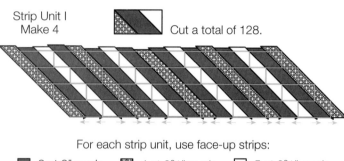

Strip Unit I
Make 4

Cut a total of 128.

For each strip unit, use face-up strips:

■ 8 at 2" mark   ▦ 4 at 2¾" mark   □ 5 at 2¾" mark

2. Assemble 4 Strip Unit II. Cut a total of 128 striped rectangles, each 2¹⁄₂" x 4¹⁄₂", from Strip Unit II. Set aside 32 striped rectangles for the pieced border.

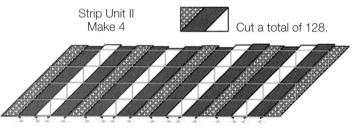

Strip Unit II
Make 4

Cut a total of 128.

For each strip unit, use face-down strips:

■ 8 at 2" mark   ▦ 4 at 2¾" mark   □ 5 at 2¾" mark

3. Using 96 striped rectangles from Strip Unit I and 96 striped rectangles from Strip Unit II, assemble 48 zigzag units. Please note that the seam allowances in the A units are pressed in a different manner than the seam allowances in the B units. This is critical for easier construction later in the block assembly.

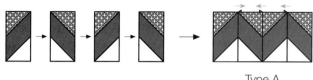

Type A
Make 24

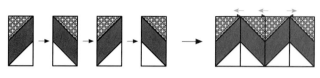

Type B
Make 24

4. Cut 2 reserved 12" dark red corner triangles and 2 reserved 12" medium red corner triangles into bias strips at the 2¾" mark. See "Reusing Method Two Corner Triangles" on page 22.

5. Assemble 2 Strip Unit III. Press 1 strip unit toward the dark red and the other toward the medium red. Cut 48 bias squares, each 2¹⁄₂" x 2¹⁄₂", from each strip unit so there are 48 pressed toward the dark red and 48 pressed toward the medium red.

Strip Unit III
Make 2
Press one strip unit toward dark red.
Press one strip unit toward medium red.   Cut 48   Cut 48

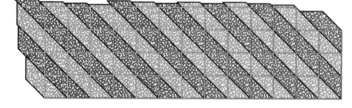

For each strip unit, use face-up strips:

▦ 5 at 2¾" mark   ▦ 5 at 2¾" mark

plus corner bias strips from step 4

6. Cut 2 reserved 12" medium green corner triangles and 2 reserved 12" dark red corner triangles into bias strips at the 2¾" mark. See "Reusing Method Two Corner Triangles" on page 22.

■ Dark green   ▨ Medium green   Light floral   □ Tan   Dark red   Medium red

7. Assemble 2 Strip Unit IV. Press 1 strip unit toward the dark red and the other toward the medium green. Cut 48 bias squares, each 2½" x 2½", from each strip unit so there are 48 pressed toward the dark red and 48 pressed toward the medium green.

Strip Unit IV
Make 2
Press one strip unit toward dark red.
Press one strip unit toward medium green.

Cut 48 Cut 48

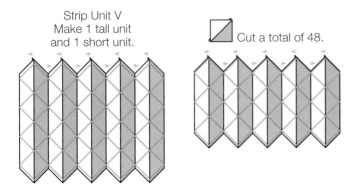

For each strip unit, use face-up strips:

5 at 2¾" mark   5 at 2¾" mark

plus corner bias strips from step 6

8. Cut the 12" medium green square once diagonally to yield 2 triangles. Stack these with the remaining 3 reserved medium green 12" triangles. Pair each medium green triangle with a reserved 12" tan triangle, placing right sides together and aligning the long edges. Cut the triangle pairs into Method One bias strips at the 2¾" mark. See page 22. You will have 1 tall and 1 short pair of strips from each triangle pair.

9. Sew pairs of bias strips on their long edges and join the same-length pairs together to make 1 tall and 1 short Strip Unit V. Cut a total of 48 bias squares, each 2½" x 2½", from Strip Unit V.

Strip Unit V
Make 1 tall unit
and 1 short unit.

Cut a total of 48.

10. Cut 2 medium red 12" squares once diagonally to yield 4 triangles. Add the remaining reserved medium red corner triangle to the stack. Pair each

medium red triangle with a reserved dark green triangle, placing right sides together and aligning the long edges. Cut the triangle pairs into Method One bias strips at the 2¾" mark. See page 22. You will have 1 tall and 1 short pair of strips from each triangle pair.

11. Sew pairs of bias strips on their long edges and join the same-length pairs together to make 1 tall and 1 short Strip Unit VI. Cut a total of 48 bias squares, each 2½" x 2½", from Strip Unit VI.

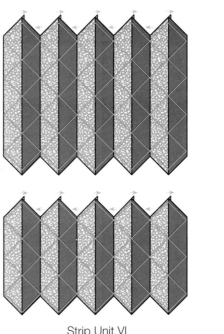

Strip Unit VI
Make 1 tall unit and 1 short unit.

Cut a total of 48.

12. Sew the dark red/medium green bias squares into pairs. Use bias squares with their seams pressed in opposite directions for each pair.

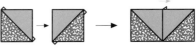

Make 48

13. Sew a pair of dark red/medium green bias squares to opposite sides of a 4½" medium red square.

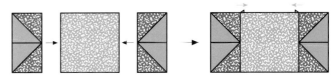

Make 12

 Dark green   Medium green   Light floral   Tan   Dark red   Medium red

14. Sew a medium green/tan bias square to opposite ends of the remaining dark red/medium green bias-square pairs.

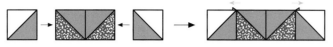

Make 24

15. Sew a unit made in step 14 to opposite sides of a unit made in step 13 to make a block center.

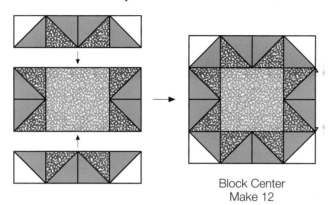

Block Center
Make 12

16. Sew a Type B zigzag unit to opposite sides of a block center to make a center row.

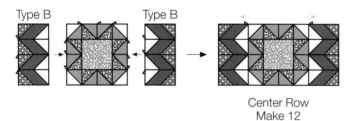

Center Row
Make 12

17. Join a 2½" medium green square, a dark green/medium red bias square, and 2 dark red/medium red bias squares to make a corner unit.

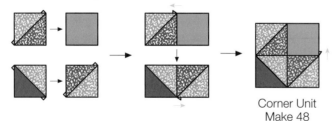

Corner Unit
Make 48

18. Sew a corner unit to opposite ends of a Type A zigzag unit to make an outer row.

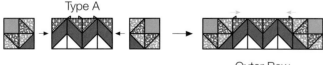

Outer Row
Make 24

19. Sew an outer row to opposite sides of a center row to complete a Fences block.

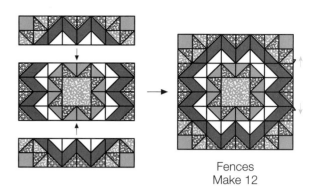

Fences
Make 12

ASSEMBLING AND FINISHING THE QUILT TOP

1. Arrange the blocks in 4 rows of 3 blocks each, alternating the final seams of each block.

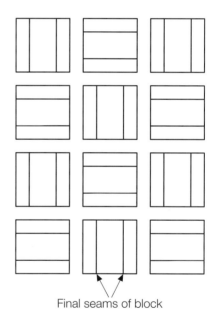

Final seams of block

2. Sew the blocks together in horizontal rows. Press the seams in opposite directions from row to row. Join the rows; press seams in either direction.

3. Attach the 2½"-wide light floral border to the quilt top, following the directions for "Plain Borders" on page 95. Press seams toward the light floral border.

■ Dark green   ■ Medium green   ▨ Light floral   □ Tan   ▨ Dark red   ▨ Medium red

4. Assemble 1 Strip Unit VII. Cut 28 striped rectangles, each 2½" x 4½", from Strip Unit VII.

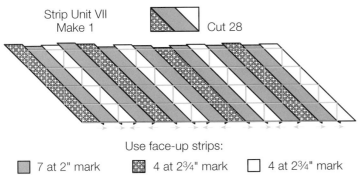

Strip Unit VII
Make 1

Cut 28

Use face-up strips:

☐ 7 at 2" mark   ☐ 4 at 2¾" mark   ☐ 4 at 2¾" mark

5. Assemble 1 Strip Unit VIII. Cut 28 striped rectangles, each 2½" x 4½", from Strip Unit VIII.

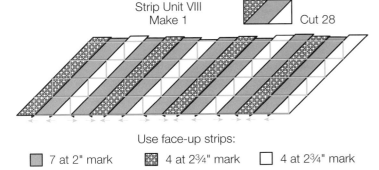

Strip Unit VIII
Make 1

Cut 28

Use face-up strips:

☐ 7 at 2" mark   ☐ 4 at 2¾" mark   ☐ 4 at 2¾" mark

6. Using 32 Strip Unit I striped rectangles, 32 Strip Unit II striped rectangles, 28 Strip Unit VII striped rectangles, and 28 Strip Unit VIII striped rectangles, make the following 4 types of units.

Center Unit
Make 4

End Unit
Make 8

Left Unit
Make 24

Right Unit
Make 24

7. Cut 4 squares, each 2½" x 2½", from the remaining reserved dark green corner triangles. Draw a line from corner to corner on the wrong side of each 2½" square. Use a fine-line mechanical pencil and sandpaper board to keep the fabric from shifting while marking. See page 6 for making a sandpaper board.

8. With right sides together, place a marked dark green square on one corner of a 4½" tan square. Pin in place and sew on the pencil line. Fold the dark green corner over the tan corner to check for accuracy. Adjust and restitch if necessary. Trim away excess

fabric ¼" from the sewing line. Press seam toward the dark green triangle.

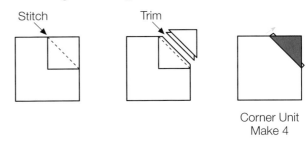

Stitch

Trim

Corner Unit
Make 4

9. Sew 7 left units together. Sew 7 right units together. Sew a center unit between the left and right rows; add an end unit to the ends of the row. Make 2 side borders. If your quilt top is properly sized, the pieced borders should fit perfectly. If not, you may need to take in or let out some of the seams on the pieced border to make it fit the quilt sides. See "Pieced Borders" on page 95. Adjust the border sizes if necessary and sew the pieced border strips to opposite sides of the quilt. Press seams toward the light floral border.

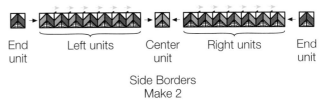

End unit   Left units   Center unit   Right units   End unit

Side Borders
Make 2

10. Sew 5 left units together. Sew 5 right units together. Sew a center unit between the left and right rows. Sew an end unit to the ends of the row; then add a corner unit to each end. Make 1 row for each of the top and bottom borders. Check the size of the border strips for accuracy as in step 9 and adjust if necessary. Sew the borders to the top and bottom of the quilt and press seams toward the light floral border.

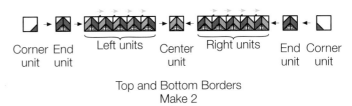

Corner unit   End unit   Left units   Center unit   Right units   End unit   Corner unit

Top and Bottom Borders
Make 2

11. Attach the 3½"-wide tan border to the quilt top, following the directions for "Plain Borders" on page 95. Repeat for the 6½"-wide dark green border.

12. Refer to the general directions for quilt finishing, beginning on page 95. Layer the completed quilt top with batting and backing; baste. Quilt as desired. Bind the edges of the quilt. Label the quilt.

 Dark green   Medium green   Light floral   Tan   Dark red   Medium red

ROYAL BEAUTY

COLOR PHOTO
ON PAGE 79

FINISHED QUILT SIZE
91¼" x 91¼"

FINISHED BLOCK SIZE
16" x 16"

Royal Beauty

⊠ Large purple print

▦ Pink print

■ Dark purple print

▨ Med.-dark purple print

▨ Med. purple print

▨ Light purple print

▨ Dark green print

▨ Med. green print

⬚ Lavender print

☐ Background print

MATERIALS: 44"-WIDE FABRIC

2½ yds. large-scale purple print for border and block centers
1¼ yds. pink print
1⅛ yds. dark purple print
¾ yd. medium-dark purple print
¾ yd. medium purple print
¾ yd. light purple print
½ yd. dark green print
⅝ yd. medium green print
1⅝ yds. lavender print for side triangles
2⅜ yds. background print
⅝ yd. binding
8¼ yds. backing

CUTTING

From the large-scale purple print, cut:
2 strips, each 4½" x 42"; crosscut into:
    13 squares, each 4½" x 4½", for block centers
9 strips, each 8½" x 42", for outer border

From the pink print, cut:
2 pieces, each 9½" x 42", for Strip Units IV and V
8 strips, each 2½" x 42", for inner border

From the dark purple print, cut:
2 pieces, each 9½" x 42", for Strip Units IV and V
10 strips, each 1½" x 42"; crosscut into:
    18 strips, each 1½" x 16½", for sashings
    2 strips, each 1½" x 18½", for sashings

From *each* of the medium-dark purple, medium purple, and light purple prints, cut:
2 pieces, each 9½" x 42", for Strip Units IV and V

From the dark green print, cut:
4 strips, each 2½" x 42"; crosscut into:
    7 strips, each 2½" x 21", for Strip Unit I

From the medium green print, cut:
7 strips, each 2½" x 42"; crosscut into:
    14 strips, each 2½" x 21", for Strip Units II and III

From the lavender print, cut:
2 squares, each 25" x 25", for side triangles
2 squares, each 14½" x 14½", for corner triangles

From the background print, cut:
2 pieces, each 9½" x 42", for Strip Units IV and V
1 piece, 9½" x 42"; crosscut into:
    2 pieces, each 9½" x 20", for Strip Units IV
    and V
7 strips, each 4½" x 42"; crosscut into:
    14 strips, each 4½" x 21", for Strip Units I and III
7 strips, each 2½" x 42"; crosscut into:
    14 strips, each 2½" x 21", for Strip Unit II

From the fabric for binding, cut:
9 strips, each 2" x 42"

Bias Strip Cutting Chart

Refer to the instructions on page 19 for cutting Method Two bias strips.

Using the Bias Stripper, cut the size and number of full bias strips indicated in the chart. Set aside leftover corner triangles for a pieced backing or another project.

FABRIC	SIZE	FABRIC DIRECTION	CUTTING MARK	NO. FULL BIAS STRIPS	STRIP UNIT
Pink	9½" x 42"	face up	2¾"	9	IV
	9½" x 42"	face down	2¾"	9	V
Dk. purple	9½" x 42"	face up	1"	18	IV
	9½" x 42"	face down	1"	18	V
Med. dark purple	9½" x 42"	face up	1"	18	IV
	9½" x 42"	face down	1"	18	V
Med. purple	9½" x 42"	face up	1"	18	IV
	9½" x 42"	face down	1"	18	V
Lt. purple	9½" x 42"	face up	1"	18	IV
	9½" x 42"	face down	1"	18	V
Background	9½" x 42"	face up	2¾"	9	IV
	9½" x 20"	face up	2¾"	3	IV
	9½" x 42"	face down	2¾"	9	V
	9½" x 20"	face down	2¾"	3	V

 Large purple   Pink   Dark purple   Medium-dark purple   Medium purple   Light purple   Dark green   Medium green   Lavender   Background

PIECING THE BLOCKS

Refer to the instructions on pages 19–21 for making striped rectangles. Press seam allowances in the direction of the arrows unless otherwise instructed.

Please note that you cannot use the BiRangle ruler to cut the striped rectangles for this quilt since they are not true rectangles, but rather striped bars.

1. Assemble 7 each of Strip Units I, II, and III. Cut a total of 52 segments, each 2½" wide, from each type of strip unit.

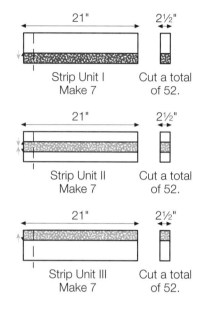

Strip Unit I
Make 7

Cut a total of 52.

Strip Unit II
Make 7

Cut a total of 52.

Strip Unit III
Make 7

Cut a total of 52.

2. Sew 1 segment from each strip unit together to make a corner unit.

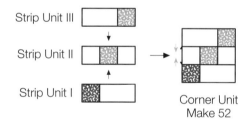

Strip Unit III

Strip Unit II

Strip Unit I

Corner Unit
Make 52

3. Assemble 3 Strip Unit IV. Cut a total of 52 striped rectangles, each 2½" x 6½", from Strip Unit IV.

Strip Unit IV
Make 3

Cut a total of 52.

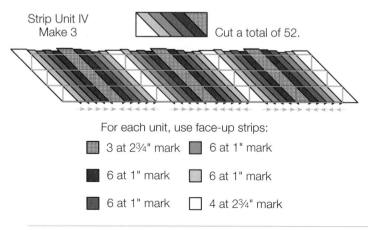

For each unit, use face-up strips:

3 at 2¾" mark   6 at 1" mark

6 at 1" mark   6 at 1" mark

6 at 1" mark   4 at 2¾" mark

4. Assemble 3 Strip Unit V. Cut a total of 52 striped rectangles, each 2½" x 6½", from Strip Unit V.

Strip Unit V
Make 3

Cut a total of 52.

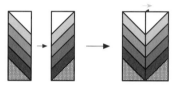

For each unit, use face-down strips:

3 at 2¾" mark   6 at 1" mark

6 at 1" mark   6 at 1" mark

6 at 1" mark   4 at 2¾" mark

5. Sew the striped rectangles from Strip Units IV and V into pairs.

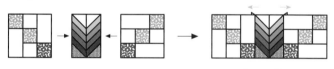

Make 52

6. Sew a corner unit to opposite sides of a rectangle pair to make an outer row.

Outer Row
Make 26

7. Sew a rectangle pair to opposite sides of a 4½" large-scale purple print square to make a center row.

Center Row
Make 13

8. Sew an outer row to opposite sides of a center row to complete a Royal Beauty block.

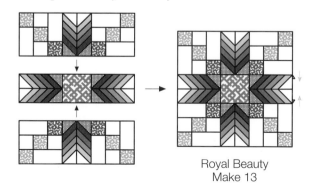

Royal Beauty
Make 13

 Large purple   Pink   Dark purple   Medium-dark purple   Medium purple   Light purple   Dark green   Medium green   Lavender   Background

ASSEMBLING AND FINISHING THE QUILT TOP

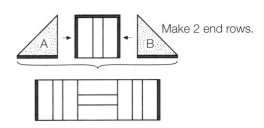

Make 2 end rows.

1. Sew a 1½" x 16½" dark purple sashing strip to opposite sides of a block. Be sure to orient the 2 final seams on the block as shown. Sew a 1½" x 18½" sashing strip to the top of the sashed block.

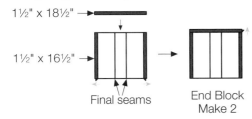

1½" x 18½"

1½" x 16½"

Final seams

End Block
Make 2

2. Sew 3 blocks together, orienting the final seams as shown. Sew a 1½" x 16½" sashing strip to each end of the row.

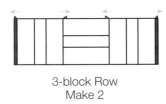

3-block Row
Make 2

3. Sew 5 blocks together, orienting the final seams as shown, to make the center row. Sew a 1½" x 16½" sashing strip to each end of the center row.

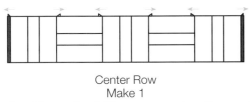

Center Row
Make 1

4. Cut the 2 lavender 25" squares twice diagonally to yield 8 quarter-square side triangles. These triangles are oversized and will be trimmed later.

5. Sew a 1½" x 16½" sashing strip to a short side of a lavender triangle to make A and B side triangles. When sewing the sashing in place, match the sashing strip with the corner.

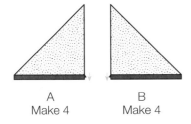

A
Make 4

B
Make 4

6. Sew an A and a B side triangle to opposite sides of an end block to make an end row. Make 2 end rows. Sew each end row to a 3-block row. Press seams in either direction.

7. Sew an A and B side triangle to opposite sides of a unit from step 6. Press seams toward triangles.

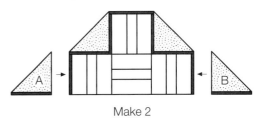

A

B

Make 2

8. Sew a unit from step 7 to opposite sides of a center row. Press seams in either direction.

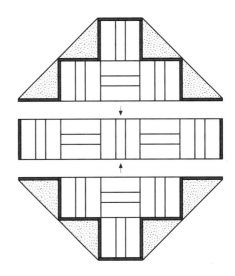

9. Cut the 14½" lavender squares once diagonally to yield 4 half-square corner triangles. Sew a corner triangle to each corner of the quilt top by centering them over the corners and stitching. Press seams toward the corner triangle. Trim the edges of the quilt top to ¼" from the sashing corners. See page 95 for information on trimming the quilt top.

10. Attach the 2½"-wide pink inner border to the quilt top, following the directions for "Plain Borders" on page 95. Repeat for the 8½"-wide large-scale purple outer border.

11. Refer to the general directions for quilt finishing, beginning on page 95. Layer the completed quilt top with batting and backing; baste. Quilt as desired. Bind the edges of the quilt. Label the quilt.

 Large purple   Pink   Dark purple   Medium-dark purple   Medium purple   Light purple   Dark green   Medium green   Lavender   Background

COLOR PHOTO
ON PAGE 80.

FINISHED QUILT SIZE
63" x 87"

FINISHED BLOCK SIZE
6" x 6"

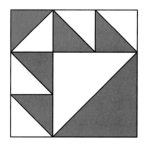

Sawtooth Square

If you've made more than one of the quilts in this book, you have no doubt noticed the instruction to "set aside leftover corner triangles for a pieced backing or another project." So, here is another project. Any pattern that uses bias squares is a good candidate for "another project," but I wanted to provide an easy design that uses up those leftovers.

Crossing Paths is made with the traditional Sawtooth Square block and uses leftover corner triangles from the patterns in this and other books of mine. Even if you don't have time right now to make an entire quilt from scraps, you can make a few blocks whenever you generate some leftovers, set them aside, and put together a quilt later when you have enough blocks.

If you don't have many leftovers, you can make "leftovers" by cutting assorted dark and light 9" squares in half on the diagonal. Instructions are given for the size of the quilt in the diagram but you are free, of course, to make any size quilt that you wish. Have fun!

MATERIALS FOR BORDERS: 44"-WIDE FABRIC

$\frac{1}{2}$ yd. for inner border
$\frac{1}{4}$ yd. for middle border
$1\frac{1}{8}$ yds. for outer border

MAKING THE BIAS SQUARES

For *each* Sawtooth Square block, you need:
5 bias squares, each $2\frac{1}{2}$" x $2\frac{1}{2}$"
1 bias square, $4\frac{1}{2}$" x $4\frac{1}{2}$"
For the entire quilt, you need:
480 bias squares, each $2\frac{1}{2}$" x $2\frac{1}{2}$"
96 bias squares, each $4\frac{1}{2}$" x $4\frac{1}{2}$"

Before beginning, please review steps 1 and 2 of "Reusing Method Two Corner Triangles" on page 22. Since you are working with leftovers, it is difficult to predict the number of bias squares you will get from what you have. You will simply have to cut the bias squares in the two sizes until you get the number required for the Crossing Paths quilt, or for the quilt size you are making. Following are a few guidelines on how to proceed.

1. Sort the corner triangles into 2 stacks of similar size: those larger than 9" on the short sides in one stack, and those smaller than 9" on the short sides in a second stack. Then within each stack, sort the fabrics into piles of darks and lights. Within each size group, pair each dark corner piece with a light corner piece, placing right sides together and aligning the bias edges and one short side. One set of narrow points should be matched so the bias strips will be even on one end. The other end will probably be uneven and ragged.

2. Beginning with a pair of corner triangles that is less than 9", cut the corner triangles into 1 pair of bias strips at the $4\frac{3}{4}$" mark.

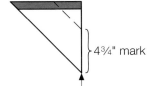

$4\frac{3}{4}$" mark

Align bias edges and 1 short side
so points are matched on one end.

3. Sew the bias-strip pair together on their long edges. Don't worry if the edges on one end are ragged and uneven. Cut a $4\frac{1}{2}$" bias square from the even end

of the strip unit. If the bias-strip pair is tall enough, you may be able to cut a $2\frac{1}{2}$" bias square from the top of the unit.

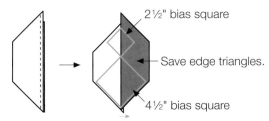

$2\frac{1}{2}$" bias square
Save edge triangles.
$4\frac{1}{2}$" bias square

Note: The edge triangles can be resized, sewn on the long edges, and cut into $2\frac{1}{2}$" bias squares. See page 9 for "Cutting Half-Square Triangles."

4. Follow the same procedure until you have all the $4\frac{1}{2}$" bias squares you need (96 for the sample quilt) or until you run out of smaller corner triangles (under 9"). If you need more $4\frac{1}{2}$" bias squares, proceed to step 5. If you have all the $4\frac{1}{2}$" bias squares you need and still have more pairs of corner triangles under 9", skip to step 7.

5. If you have run out of dark/light corner triangles under 9" but still need more $4\frac{1}{2}$" bias squares, begin using the larger pairs of corner triangles. Cut a pair of large corner triangles into 1 pair of bias strips at the $2\frac{3}{4}$" mark. Sew the strips together on the long edges and press the seams toward the dark. Reserve them for step 8.

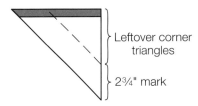

Leftover corner triangles
$2\frac{3}{4}$" mark

Cut this way if you need
large bias squares.

6. Sew the leftover pair of corner triangles together on their long edges. Cut one $4\frac{1}{2}$" bias square from the unit. Continue in this fashion until you have all the $4\frac{1}{2}$" bias squares you need.

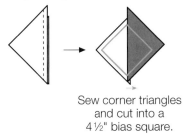

Sew corner triangles
and cut into a
$4\frac{1}{2}$" bias square.

7. Now that you are done making $4\frac{1}{2}$" bias squares, you can continue making $2\frac{1}{2}$" bias squares exclusively. You need 480 for the Crossing Paths quilt.

Cut any size pair of corner triangles (over or under 9") into bias strips at the 2¾" mark.

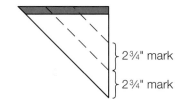

2¾" mark

2¾" mark

Cut this way if you do not need
more large bias squares.

8. Sew the pairs of strips together on their long edges; press seams toward the dark strip. Sew these plus any 2¾" bias-strip pairs from step 5 into 1 large multiple bias strip unit. Align the even ends of the strip pairs on one side of the strip unit and the ragged ones on the other. Intermix the different prints in the strip unit for a scrappier look.

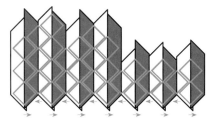

Keep points aligned
on one side of strip
unit. Begin cutting
from this side.

9. Working from the even side of the unit, cut as many 2½" bias squares from the strip unit as you can. Remember, the edge triangles can be resized and sewn into 2½" bias squares, too. Continue making multiple bias strip units and cutting bias squares until you have as many 2½" bias squares as you need for the quilt you are making.

PIECING A BLOCK

Press seam allowances in the direction of the arrows unless otherwise instructed.

1. Sew five 2½" bias squares and one 4½" bias square, as shown, to make a Sawtooth Square block. Make 96 for the Crossing Paths quilt, or as many as you need for the quilt you are making.

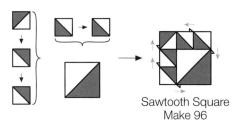

Sawtooth Square
Make 96

2. Sew 4 Sawtooth Square blocks together as shown to make one large block.

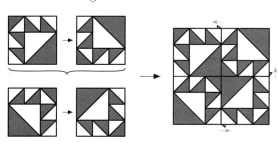

ASSEMBLING AND FINISHING THE QUILT TOP

1. Arrange the large blocks into 6 rows of 4 blocks each, rotating the blocks as necessary to create Rows A and B.

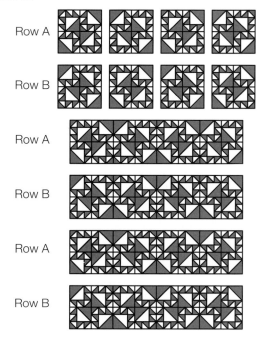

Row A

Row B

Row A

Row B

Row A

Row B

2. Sew the blocks in horizontal rows. Press seams in opposite directions from row to row. Join the rows. Press seams in either direction.

3. For border, cut:
   6 strips, each 2" x 42", for inner borders
   7 strips, each 1" x 42", for middle borders
   7 strips, each 5" x 42", for outer borders
   Attach the 2"-wide inner border to the quilt top, following the directions for "Plain Borders" on page 95. Repeat for the middle and outer borders.

4. Refer to the general directions for quilt finishing, beginning on page 95. Layer the completed quilt top with batting and backing; baste. Quilt as desired. Bind the edges of the quilt. Label the quilt.

Quilt Finishing

Once your quilt top is done, you'll be anxious to finish your quilt. The following information is a brief overview of the basics. The Joy of Quilting series of books from That Patchwork Place addresses in depth each aspect of quiltmaking. I strongly encourage you to review them for more extensive ideas on machine and hand quilting, setting quilts together, and binding.

ADDING BORDERS

Straighten the edges of the quilt top before adding the borders. There should be little or no trimming needed for a straight-set quilt. A diagonally set quilt is often constructed with oversized side triangles, and you may need to trim these down to size. Align the ¼" line on the ruler with the block points and trim the quilt edges to ¼" from these points. Always position a ¼" line of the ruler along the block points of the adjacent edge at the same time, so that the corner will be square when the trimming has been completed.

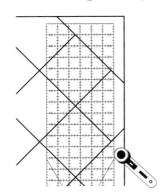

Trim the edges of the quilt to ¼" from the block points.

PLAIN BORDERS

To find the correct measurement for plain border strips, always measure through the center of the quilt, not at the outside edges. This ensures that the borders are of equal length on opposite sides of the quilt and brings the outer edges into line with the center dimension if discrepancies exist. Otherwise, your quilt might not be "square," due to minor piecing errors and/or stretching that can occur while you work with the pieces.

Center length

1. Measure the quilt from the top to the bottom edge through the center of the quilt. Cut two border strips to this measurement, piecing as necessary, and pin them to the sides of the quilt, easing to fit as necessary.

Note: If there is a large difference in the two sides or between the center and the sides, it is better to go back and correct the source of the problem now rather than try to make the border fit and end up with a distorted quilt later.

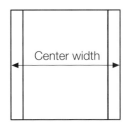
Center width

2. Sew the side borders in place and press the seams toward the borders.
3. Measure the center width of the quilt, including the side borders, to determine the length of the top and bottom border strips. Cut the borders to this measurement, piecing as necessary, and pin them to the top and bottom of the quilt top, again easing to fit as needed. Stitch in place and press the seams toward the border strips.

PIECED BORDERS

It is easiest to apply pieced borders to quilt tops that are the proper size. If the quilt top is considerably different in size than it should be, it may be best to recalculate the number of pieced units to be used in the border or eliminate the pieced border altogether. Small differences in size can usually be accommodated.

1. Measure the center length of the quilt top. Measure the length of the pieced borders that will go on the sides of the quilt top. If they match, pin and sew the pieced borders to the sides of the quilt top, positioning any seams that need to be aligned with quilt-top seams. If there is a slight difference in the sizes of the borders and quilt sides, take in or let out a little from several seams on the pieced borders until they fit the dimensions of the quilt sides. Do not take in or let out only one seam or its difference in size will be very noticeable. A tiny adjustment in many seams will go unnoticed.
2. Follow the same procedure to measure the width of the quilt and to adjust and sew the top and bottom borders in place.

CHOOSING AND MARKING QUILTING DESIGNS

Quilting serves several purposes, the most important being to hold the three layers of the quilt together. Therefore, it is important to do an adequate amount of quilting, whether by hand or machine, to serve this purpose. The density of the quilting should be consistent so that one area of the quilt does not pucker or bulge as a result of too little or too much quilting. Keep this in mind when choosing your quilt designs—a heavily quilted border will also require heavy quilting in the interior.

There are a tremendous number of sources for quilting designs available commercially. Stencils are immensely popular and readily available. It's a simple matter to trace through the lines to mark the design you want. Other books deal exclusively with drawings of quilt designs that can be transferred in various ways to the quilt top. Simple overall designs such as crosshatching, quilting in-the-ditch, outline quilting, and echo quilting are time-honored methods of quilting that do not require commercial stencils and books. Of course, you are free to design your own, too.

Many quilting designs must be marked directly on the quilt top to act as an accurate guide for your stitches. Choose nonpermanent markers for this task—I have seen the beauty of many a quilt ruined by permanent quilt markings. There is a wonderful assortment of wash-out markers available today. With all the time and expense put into the quilt top, it's a comparatively small expense to spend a few dollars on a good marker. Be sure to test a new marker on scrap fabric for washability before using it on your quilt top.

Before marking, press the quilt top one final time. Mark on a hard flat surface, keeping your marker sharp and your lines clear and fine. It's best to mark the quilt top all at one time, but sometimes it is not possible, and you may need to mark your top as you quilt. If this is the case, do your best to keep the lines from smudging as you will be marking on a padded surface.

MAKING A QUILT BACKING

The quilt backing is sometimes called the lining. It is the back of the quilt. It must be cut 3" to 4" wider than the quilt top on all sides to allow for any shifting during the quilting process. To determine the size of the quilt backing you need, whether plain or pieced, measure the finished quilt top and add 6" to both length and width. For example, a quilt top that measures 38" x 54" requires a 44" x 60" backing.

The simplest quilt backings to make are plain backings. Many hand quilters prefer this type because there aren't any seams to quilt through. A plain backing is one piece of fabric without any seams. Plain or printed muslins are available in a number of different widths to accommodate all but the largest-size quilts. Choose a width larger than the width of the quilt backing to allow for shrinkage. To figure how many yards you need, convert the quilt-backing length to yards (divide by 36). Round this figure up to the nearest $1/8$ yard and add another $1/8$ yard for shrinkage. Purchase this amount.

A paneled backing is similar to a plain backing except that it is pieced in one or two vertical panels. The patterns in this book contain yardage to make paneled backings, using standard 44"-wide fabric that shrinks to approximately 42". If your quilt backing measures over 42" wide, then you need two panels. Three panels are needed for a quilt backing over 84" wide. Figure yardage by doubling or tripling the quilt-backing length, depending on the number of panels needed. Divide this figure by 36, round up to the nearest $1/8$ yard, and add another $1/8$ yard for shrinkage.

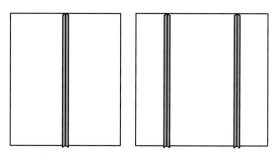

Two ways to piece paneled backings

An increasingly popular and fun way to make a quilt backing is to piece one. It can be pieced from large squares, triangles, rectangles, and "mistakes" left over from the quilt top or even other coordinating prints that you have on hand. No matter what you do, it is considerably less expensive, uses leftovers, and is totally delightful to discover on the back of a quilt. There are two examples of pieced backings in the Gallery.

BASTING THE QUILT LAYERS

The quilt sandwich is composed of the quilt top, backing, and a filler material called the batting. There are many battings available in both synthetic and natural fibers. Entire books are devoted to the advantages and disadvantages of the different types. Whatever batting you choose, be sure to read and follow the manufacturer's instructions on any preparation that may need to be done. The batting should be the same size as your backing. I open packaged batting and lay it flat and covered (I have cats!) on a bed overnight to relax the wrinkles and creases.

Once the quilting designs are marked, the backing made, and a batting bought and prepared, you are ready to secure the three layers with basting. Press the backing smooth and tape it, right sides down, to a hard, clean, flat work surface, such as a table or floor. Do not use a surface that you don't want marred with pin marks! Securely tape the sides of the backing every few inches. Tape the corners last, being careful not to stretch the bias. Smooth and center the batting over the backing. Carefully place the quilt top over the batting right side up. Smooth it and begin pin basting it to the other layers, always working from the center out. This will work out any unevenness in the layers.

For hand quilting, use a light-colored thread to baste the sandwich in a 3" to 4" grid, again working from the center out. Baste across both diagonals of the sandwich to stabilize the bias. Finish by securing the edges of the quilt sandwich with a line of stitches around the edge. Remove the pins.

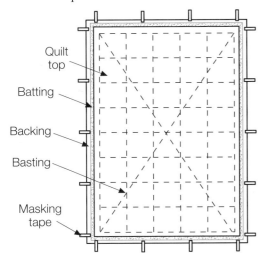

Quilt top
Batting
Backing
Basting
Masking tape

Many machine quilters and even some hand quilters prefer special quilter's safety pins to baste the sandwich instead of thread. Recently, some quilters have begun to use plastic tacks such as those used to secure price tags to clothing. They are available at quilt and hobby shops or through mail-order catalogs.

QUILTING

I have no expertise in machine quilting and recommend you refer to books by experts in that field for how-to information. I do hand quilt, though, and will briefly review the basics.

Quilting is a simple running stitch that goes through all three layers of the quilt sandwich. All quilting should be done from the center out. Most quilters prefer to use some type of frame to hold the three layers together when quilting to prevent them from shifting.

Quilting needles are called Betweens and come in different sizes. The larger the number, the smaller the needle and the smaller your stitches. Try to use the smallest needle you can comfortably handle. The eyes are tiny, so many people use a needle threader to thread them. Use cotton hand-quilting thread cut into 12" to 18" lengths. Longer threads will weaken from sliding through the eye continuously. I strongly recommend that you use a thimble on your stitching finger. Some quilters also use one on the "receiving" finger under the quilt.

1. Begin quilting with a small single knot tied close to the end of the thread. Slip the needle between the layers of the quilt about a needle length's distance from your chosen starting point. If possible, weave the needle through a seam allowance. Bring the needle up where you want to start and give the thread a tug to lodge the knot in the batting or seam.

2. Following the quilting marks, sew a simple running stitch, being sure to catch all three layers with each stitch. Ideally, the stitches on the back of the quilt should be the same size as the stitches on the front. All stitches should be of consistent size and evenly spaced. This can take some practice. It is better to sacrifice small stitch size in favor of even spacing and consistent size.

3. End a line of quilting by forming a small knot in the thread about $1/8$" from where it exits the quilt. Take the last stitch between the layers only and run the needle a short distance away from the last stitch before bringing the needle up, out of the quilt. Again, weaving the thread in and out of a seam allowance before exiting will strengthen the quilting. Give a gentle tug, and the knot will slip between the layers. Clip the thread a short distance from the quilt top and let the tail slip back between the layers.

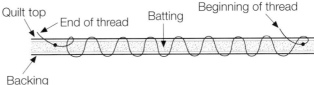

Quilt top
End of thread
Batting
Beginning of thread
Backing

4. Continue to quilt, working from the center of the quilt toward the edges to ease out any fullness. Finish all the quilting and remove the interior basting stitches before binding the quilt. Leave the perimeter basting stitches in place to hold the edges for the binding.

Binding the Quilt

The fabric requirements for the patterns in this book are based on cutting straight-of-grain fabric strips for a double-fold binding. This is a simple but durable binding.

Note: If you want to attach a sleeve or rod pocket to the back of the quilt, see page 99 for making the sleeve before you attach the binding.

1. Cut 2"-wide strips from selvage to selvage for a standard ¼"-wide finished binding.
2. Join the strips at right angles and stitch across the corner. Make one long piece of binding. Trim excess fabric and press seams open. It is important to use closely matching threads in this situation to avoid peekaboo stitches at the seams.

3. Fold the strip in half lengthwise, wrong sides together, and press. At one end of the strip, turn under ¼" at a 45° angle and press.

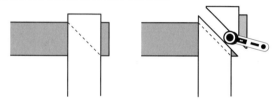

Fold line

To attach the binding:
1. Baste the three layers of the quilt securely at the outer edges if you have not already done so.
2. Trim the batting and backing even with the quilt top edges and corners if necessary.
3. In the center of one edge of the quilt, align the raw edges of the binding with the raw edge of the quilt top. Leaving about 6" free as a starting tail, sew the binding to the edge of the quilt with a ¼"-wide seam allowance. Stop stitching ¼" from the corner of the first side. (It's a good idea to pin-mark ¼" in from the corner before you begin sewing.) Backstitch and remove the quilt from the machine.

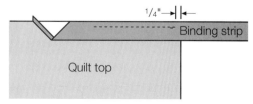

¼"→| |←
Binding strip
Quilt top

4. To create a neat, mitered turn at the corner, flip the binding straight up from the corner so that it forms a continuous line with the adjacent side of the quilt top.

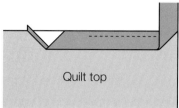

Quilt top

5. Fold the binding straight down so it lies on top of the adjacent side, being careful not to shift the pleat formed at the fold. Pin the pleat in place. Pin-mark ¼" in from the next corner. Starting at the edge, stitch the second side of the binding to the quilt, stopping at the ¼" mark. Flip up, then down, repeating the same process for the remaining corners.

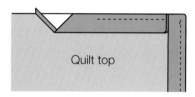

Quilt top

6. Repeat on the remaining edges and corners of the quilt. When you reach the beginning of the binding, overlap the beginning stitches by about 1" and cut away any excess binding, trimming the end at a 45° angle. Tuck the end of the binding into the fold and finish the seam.

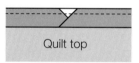

Quilt top

7. Turn the binding to the back of the quilt. Slipstitch the fold of the binding to the quilt backing. Slipstitch the miters in place on both front and back to complete the binding—and your quilt!

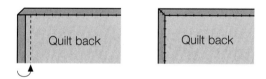

Quilt back   Quilt back

ADDING A SLEEVE

You will need to add a hanging sleeve if you plan to display your finished quilt on the wall.

1. Using leftover fabric or a piece of muslin, cut a strip 6" to 8" wide and 1" shorter than the width of the quilt at the top edge. Fold the ends under ½", then ½" again, and stitch.

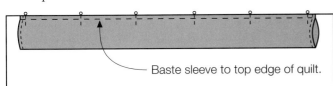

2. Fold the fabric strip in half lengthwise, wrong sides together, and baste the raw edges to the top edge of the back of your quilt. The top edge of the sleeve will be secured when the binding is sewn onto the quilt.

Baste sleeve to top edge of quilt.

3. Finish the sleeve after the binding has been attached by blindstitching the bottom of the sleeve in place. Push the bottom edge of the sleeve up just a bit to provide a little give so the hanging rod does not put strain on the quilt itself.

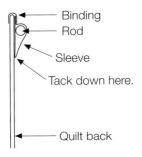

Binding
Rod
Sleeve
Tack down here.
Quilt back

LABELING YOUR QUILT

Be sure to sign and date your quilt. Labels can be elaborate or simple, and can be handwritten, typed, or embroidered. Be sure to include the name of the quilt, your name, your city and state, the date, and the name of the recipient if it is a gift. Add any other interesting or important information about the quilt. Future generations will be interested to know more about the quilt than just who made it and when.

About the Author

Born and raised in southeastern Pennsylvania, Donna started using a needle when she was four years old. Her mother was a home economics teacher and her father an engineer. It seems only natural, then, that Donna, with a love of fabric and stitching and a passion for geometry and math, would take to quilting.

Donna has been quilting since 1975 and teaching since 1982, earning her National Quilting Association teacher's certification in 1988. The introduction of rotary-cutting tools in the early 1980s revolutionized her approach to quiltmaking. Since that time, she has worked exclusively with rotary-cut and machine-pieced quilts, from miniature to full size.

She is the author of four other books: *Small Talk* (miniature quiltmaking), *Shortcuts: A Concise Guide to Rotary Cutting*, *A Perfect Match: A Guide to Precise Machine Piecing*, and *Shortcuts to the Top* (more applications of rotary cutting). The metric version of *Shortcuts* has been translated into four languages and *Shortcuts to the Top* is co-published in a metric German translation. Donna is also a contributing author to *The Quilter's Companion: Everything You Need to Know to Make Beautiful Quilts*. In addition, she has designed a new ruler, the Bias Stripper™, that makes it possible to cut accurate, properly sized bias strips.

The Thomas family consists of Donna, her husband, Terry (whose hobby is cooking), and their two teenage sons, Joe and Peter. Terry's military career has taken them many places and, as a result, Donna has had the opportunity to teach quiltmaking in many parts of the country as well as overseas.

Having recently moved from Kansas to Peachtree City, Georgia, Donna continues to make quilts, write, teach, and pursue her other passion—gardening.

That Patchwork Place Publications and Products

4", 6", 8", & metric Bias Square® • BiRangle™ • Ruby Beholder™ • ScrapMaster • Rotary Rule™ • Rotary Mate™
Shortcuts to America's Best-Loved Quilts (video)

Many titles are available at your local quilt shop. For more information, send $2 for a color catalog to
That Patchwork Place, Inc., PO Box 118, Bothell WA 98041-0118 USA.

☎ Call 1-800-426-3126 for the name and location of the quilt shop nearest you.